Any Version of History is Just

A STORY

Saeed Al Mubarak

Any Version of History is just a STORY

Copyright

ISBN: 978-1-7346366-6-6 (Hardcover)
ISBN: 978-1-7346366-1-1 (Paperback)
ISBN: 978-1-7346366-8-0 (Electronic)

Library of Congress Control Number: 2020902848

Front cover image by:
Furqan Ahmed Qidwai

Internal artwork by:
Mahmoud Saeed Al Mubarak
Zainab Saeed Al Mubarak
Sharaf Saeed Al Mubarak

Saeed M Al Mubarak
Safwa, Saudi Arabia

Saeedalmubarak@yahoo.com
https://www.linkedin.com/in/saeedmubarak/
http://www.challengeparadigm.com

Dedication

To the most loving, caring and patient man I have ever seen,
my late father.

To the toughest woman who holds within the softest heart,
my mother.

To my sons:
the young version of me whom I wish to become better than me.

To my little princesses:
the most precious gifts of my life.

To my wife:
the queen of my heart, the love of my life and my dearest friend.

Introduction

To the Respected Readers

My late father once told me "the knowledge you have is not yours – share it." I realized that the quality of life we have today is a result of cumulative knowledge and efforts of people from different times, different cultures, and different places. Some witnessed the value of their work during their lives while most of the value of their work was seen after they were gone. Indeed, they have continued to share and care as if they were still alive. What is more precious than knowledge itself is sharing it with others; therefore, I wrote this book.

I have experienced vicissitudes in my journey in life, and I have been watching others do the same. I realized that there will always be multiple perceptions of how the world looks. Despite the strong bond between humans and their habits, history, and culture, our perceptions of the world are influenced by an ever-changing social, emotional, psychological, mental, spiritual, and moral status, as well as by what we know. We do change all the time and so do our perceptions of realities. Sadly enough, humans will always find something to fight over, though – ethnicity, skin color, tribal allegiances, etc.

So, how do we persuade humans to find harmony instead of looking for conflict, peace instead of war, love instead of hate, and tolerance instead of prejudice? There will always be good and bad in this life. What you are determined to do and focus on is relatively what you will see, react to, and what will become your unique reality. It is very hard for any of us to acknowledge that there are people who influence and possibly control how we make our most important choices in life.

You need to decide who you want to be and how you want your reality to be. The search journey for truth and enlightenment will help you distinguish between how things appear and how things really are. In this journey, it is much better to walk alone in the right direction than to follow others going in the wrong direction. It will not be an easy journey, but if you keep going, you will not only see immediate benefits but it will also be worth it in the end.

The thirty-two topics that make up this book are vaguely related, and every topic can stand alone to represent a subject. While the topics can be sequenced in many different ways, it is typical that the first article leads to the next. Most articles are introduced with a judicious story, a natural phenomenon, a scientific fact, theoretical perspectives or divine imperatives. They all end with intriguing and thought-provoking questions for you to contemplate and think about. Every article has messages waiting for you, respected reader, to uncover. You can read these articles in any order you see fit.

When writing, I like connecting the beginnings and endings. The book starts with "Any Version of History is Just a Story" and ends with "Be the Author of Your Own Story." When you approach the end of the book, you will uncover the connections between the beginning and the ending. What you may like even more is that you may read the book backwards and realize that the story of your life that you have authored will, one day, become multiple stories.

I am sure you will identify different messages every time you reread any of the articles as every rereading would seem to be reading a new article for the first time. The more you reread, the more your subconscious eliminates the distractions to discover more of the hidden treasures in the articles. The main benefits you will find in this book are to learn about the ways to examine conventional wisdoms, uncover roots of paradigms, challenge them, unlock hidden brain power, and participate in making a difference in your life and the lives of others.

Table of Contents

Any version of history is just a story
and the story might be only a shadow.

Any Version of History Is Just a STORY!

One would want to acquire knowledge of the past and the present to know the "truth" or at least understand how "truth" is perceived. In today's world, we are privileged with what the advancement in media technologies has provided and how we can easily search, explore, see, hear, or read about almost anything. One wonders why humans are too attached to and too influenced by their history – their version of history. Some people feel proud about their history, while others feel ashamed about things they can't change or influence. One may argue that the media has almost no influence on those who choose what to see or hear based on what they already believe, while others suggest that the media has a great influence in promoting biases, deception, illusions, partial truth but not the whole truth, and it only tells us what it wants to or how we should think!

People who live in the present are living histories, aren't they? These people are supposed to have first-hand experience on what is happening around the globe; they have direct access to countless live-media sources, live communication platforms, etc.

Yet, all they see and/or hear is just part of the story. For those who are visual learners, I am including the below picture to illustrate the concept.

Nowadays, there is not a unified story about what is happening around us. There is not a single version of the truth, but multiple versions. What one perceives as a truth might be just an image, an illusion, or just a shadow of an object. This image is influenced by light intensity, distance, and the direction of the "camera."

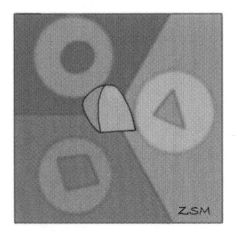

The camera operator or the director may choose an angle, a distance, and/or even some side effects, just to attract viewers. Unfortunately, all image producers have a unique set of cameras, processing procedures, and side effects that facilitate their own agenda/propaganda.

Once the story is published, it becomes (hi)STORY. Sometimes you become a producer, a cameraman, a director, and a storyteller. Other times, you are the (hi)STORY. Be aware that there might be multiple versions of your own STORY as might be the case of icons, celebrities, politicians, leaders, heroes, and historical figures.

How about the viewers?

I guess that every single viewer has a unique perception of the "truth." This perception of the truth can be based on various aspects pertaining to physical senses, beliefs, moral compass, biases, and/or other "filters," and it is processed and confirmed automatically and unconsciously. If we consider that the perceived truths in the above illustrations are the shadows of things, then definitely there will be multiple truths (i.e., shadows) in the mind of the observers who unintentionally dismiss or deliberately ignore any other possibility or evidence that may indicate otherwise. The irony is that all perceptions based on shadows are merely wrong! Yet every viewer confirms that it is the truth and may passionately defend it as if it were the only truth. It is all personalized and all mere conventions. The more people share the same convention, the more real it becomes. The more people question it, the more deceptive it becomes.

How about history itself; the history of our culture, religion, civilizations and even people– hundreds or even thousands of years ago?

One may answer: If we are incapable of determining the absolute truth about current stories, situations, social activities, behaviors, or personnel, how would we be able to uncover the absolute truth about history, especially history that has parts from it based on a shadow that may vaguely be remembered, distortedly recovered, or evilly invented. People need to realize that others view things from different perspectives, and they draw their conclusions accordingly. "Slaves of history" will never grasp your great message unless they free themselves from this slavery.

They may continue to debate, argue, and dispute about these emotionally appealing subjects even if they are provided with the absolute historical truth, if it even exists.

In a nutshell, accepting that we might not know it all, honoring that others see things differently, and recognizing that we and others might be equally wrong may lead us to become more tolerant, respectful, and kinder to others – yet different; and it is okay to be different. Do enjoy and learn from any version of history; it is just a STORY.

Challenge Yourself

- Do you think your version of history is absolutely right?
- Is it really important to know what happened (i.e., history) and what is happening? Why?
- What would be the best sources of knowledge, and how much of it is enough?

- One final important question: Would you be able to GENUINELY accept others the way they are?

No matter what society or country we belong to, there are virtues and evils that our minds give us the general right guidance to identify, and we either follow or dismiss.

How Do You Know
What's Right and What's Wrong?

One gets concerned about what's right and what's wrong, gets confused about what's just or unjust, and wonders if all we do is trade opinions.

One person may say that an action is just, while another says that the exact same action is NOT just!! It is very possible that both have a convincing argument about their opinions. An observer wonders "if there is a way to know what is just, like it is in math that 1+1=2." This truth in its abstract form is supposed to be acceptable by everyone, and it is not a matter of opinion or just appearances.

All types of math calculators will give similar results when used to calculate numbers. One could suggest inventing a "universal moral/ethics calculator" capable of calculating an objective truth; another one may not accept the concept and argue that it is not practical nor achievable. Aristotle thought that ethics are not like math; they are just a matter of making decisions using best judgments and available knowledge in order to find the right path.

One would wish that "best judgments," ethics, justice, and even "the right path" could become a lot like math with a universal approach to calculate the outcome. Unfortunately, they are not.

Haven't you ever opposed others for being "unjust"? Bring any of those situations to mind and think about it, then, evaluate your decision-making approach. Was it a gut feeling, was it a scientific approach, was it a religious cause, was it a political reason, or a financial interest? Was it your opinion or someone else's (e.g., your parents, friends, school or culture)?

The sour reality is… We all know or at least feel we know what's right or wrong, but we choose to ignore what we know in order to justify our ignorance. Every one of us has an "innate compass" that leads us in the general directions of right and wrong; we call it "conscious mind." This innate compass steers us from day-to-day dangers such as walking in front of an oncoming bus or train, or going to the doctor when we are sick. This guidance is magnified when we deal with society and other people and provides direction as well. Nobody in their "right" mind likes war and hates peace and tranquility. No sane person believes that selling narcotics is a decent act, and, for sure, nobody would like to be associated with child trafficking or abuse! The problem starts when we fool around with the raw calibration of the compass. We start giving different positive adjectives to what we do so that we go into negative ignorance as opposed to positive knowledge. We start to link wars to rewards. We claim we provide comfort for people to escape daily pressures when we sell them drugs. We continue going down on the scale of ignorance and not just participate but cheer and recruit others to participate in "negative" acts.

No matter what society or country we belong to, there are virtues and evils that our minds give us the general right guidance to identify, and we either follow or dismiss. We fool ourselves when we create positive labels for some evils and negative labels of the virtues to be convinced of the opposite.

The fall towards the bottom of ignorance is not limited, and the rise towards the top of the virtue scale is not limited either. We just need to use the raw tools that we have been provided with; unfortunately, the materialistic world has dragged humanity in the race to unlimited desires and has gradually been diminishing the influence of our "raw tools and innate compass."

The sad matter is that most evil done in this world is not done by people who choose to be evil, but by those who do not think critically enough or who are not willing to accept the inconveniences that the truth could bring.

Maybe one day, the innate compass will rise again and transform into a "universal moral calculator" and will help guide us in defining what is right and what is wrong. This universal calculator will adjust itself with changes in time, cultures, ideologies, perceptions, and life.

Every one of us possesses a "calculator" with its unique formula and possibly yielding different results. Our calculations may drift and deviate, and they will always need to be calibrated against a universal compass that is capable of resolving complex situations and disputes as easily as calculating 1+1=2.

Challenge Yourself

- What would it take to come up with a universal moral calculator?

- Prior to the invention of this calculator, how do you know what's right and what's wrong?

- How would you describe what is right and wrong to a layman or a child?

- Humans will always find something to fight over – ethnicity, skin color, tribal allegiances, etc... So, how do we persuade humans to find harmony instead of looking for conflict, peace instead of war, love instead of hate, tolerance instead of prejudice, which one of these is the main cause of tipping the balance of justice?

There will always be good and bad in this life.
What you are determined to focus on is relatively
what you will see, react to, and will become your
unique reality.
Just decide how you want your reality to be.

I Don't Know What I Don't Know

As much as it is thought-provoking, it is disturbing to envision a physical world where freedom does not exist; a world that is perceived to be governed by physical rules, borders, cause and effect, and even by unexplained "physical" phenomena. Freedom only exists beyond known finite boundaries: our physical bodies, earth, and the universe. It exists in "minds" that are not anchored to the materialistic world or influenced by limited knowledge. One may rightly assume that the common phrase "thinking out of the box" is meant to set minds free.

I developed the below illustration to graphically convey the message of an Arabic proverb that talks about four categories of men based on what they "think" they know. The proverb is as follows:

He that knows, and knows that he knows is a scholar. Follow him.

He that knows not, and knows that he knows not is an ignorant. Teach him.

He that knows, and knows not that he knows is an amnesiac. Remind him.

He that knows not, and knows not that he knows not is a fool. Shun him.

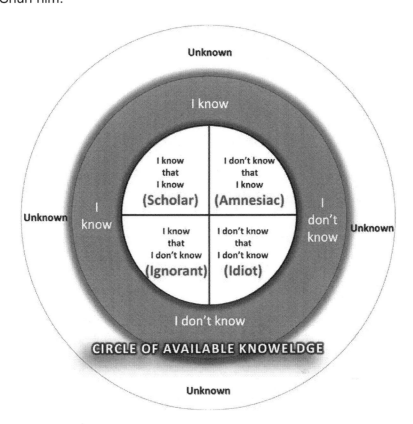

The limits or borders of the circle of accessible knowledge have not yet been found. Our finite circle of knowledge is perceived to be in a continuous expansion mode. In the expansion journey, we shall have evolutions of "truths." Newton's theories were fine and believed to be "true" until Einstein brought us the theory of relativity with the time element. What was believed to be true at certain knowledge boundaries turned out to be incomplete or true within limits. Well, Einstein's theories are being challenged by string theory, the new game in town. Soon, string theory will also be challenged.

Scientists discover thousands of new species of new animals, insects, and plants every year, and there are still more to be discovered. Moreover, scientists today are still struggling to uncover the secret about many things of an advanced nature: pyramids, coral castle, and lots of "hidden knowledge." There are many who believe that this circle of available knowledge was once much larger!

It could be that the types of science, energy, communication, and technologies, that existed once, were completely different from ours. For certain, they were not developed by primitive societies/civilizations. One could argue that those old civilizations were leaps ahead in knowledge, science, and technologies. There will always be at least two sides of the coin of knowledge, and all we know is a portion of only one side. Ignorance will often, if not always, be the twin of knowledge. The less-ignorant ones are the more certain about knowledge they possess as opposed to belief or opinion about which there are more doubts. Infallibilism may only be reached when one possesses the ultimate knowledge of all there is to know.

No one doubts the power of science and scientific approaches; yet, numerous inexplicable phenomena are yet to be explained. It may not be a limitation in science itself only, but also a limitation in how much we know. Creation, gravity, dreams, consciousness, unconsciousness, emptiness, instincts, and death are a few examples that demonstrate the struggle among great scientists, philosophers, and theologians to find a dominant explanation.

Some think that man has barely scraped the surface of all there is to know. One wonders if humans will ever possess the ultimate knowledge, whatever the ultimate knowledge is. We do not always know what we do not know. Is it meant to be this way? Perhaps not. Is it a blessing or a curse?

We don't know if what we don't know is important or insignificant, good or bad, white or black, etc.

We don't know what knowledge is, what power is, what love is, and what hate is, and even if we try to rationalize them, we don't know their limits and how they are measured. Man has been trying to explore earth, oceans, space, and even the outer universe when he is helpless to unfold the secrets of his own "universe" and does not realize that an entire cosmos is folded in him and in every single cell. Everyone is a unique, precious universe that remains to be explored for the GOOD this universe has to offer.

Some will loudly say: Who cares? Well, those who realize how little they know do care.

Those who care realize that every person perceives things in different ways, making his/her own unique reality, a "reality" that is more subjective and is influenced by the prior limited knowledge, which formulates the framework of thinking, comprehension, and communication. The levels of comprehension of a technical or a philosophical article are vastly different when it is read by an expert vs. a "layman"; that's only because of one factor: prior knowledge that includes experiences, conditioning, and belief. Why would one not be surprised about the vast spectrum of interpretations about all sort of writings, media, practices, and even cultures?

It is fascinating!

No normal person would be able to have prior knowledge about everything. A person may spend a lifetime studying and be specialized in multiple subjects, a few languages, and sciences. It is just hard and almost impossible to find individuals who possess extraordinary capacities, and although these kinds of people exist, they are not considered NORMAL!

What if, in this particular thing, they were normal but we do not see them as normal because we have already predefined what normal is? This has become our default, a default that we may consciously and freely choose to alter, rather than being emotionally attached to a belief system. So think about your "normal" – it may not be the "normal" of others.

These variations are not associated with our physical body, the vessel, or its parts. People have similar brains, heart, lungs, kidneys, and cells. Although all these spectacular and precious physical entities came out of one single origin, they have their own universes, memories, missions, and destination. All of them have the prior knowledge to function well alone and synergistically with others in bodies of those who know that they know (scholars), do not know they know (amnesiacs), know they do not know that they know (ignorants), and even for those who do not know that they do not know (idiots).

Some believe that humans are the custodians of the world! Some may dispute this belief knowing how much harm humans have caused to this precious world, let alone the harm humans have done to their own kind.

For humans to function well, the ultimate knowledge of the outer world may not be required. However, the knowledge of oneself (the inner world), mission, values, destination, and how "to function well alone and synergistically with others" is a constituent that is primed to achieve a healthy fabric of not only humanity but also the whole universe. Those who acquire the knowledge about and the focus on a peaceful, loving, and caring inner world are those who have more opportunity to expand their awareness and possess a free will.

There will always be good and bad in this life. What you are determined to do and focus on is relatively what you will see, react to, and what will become your unique reality. Just decide how you want your reality to be.

Challenge Yourself

- How do you think a culture would exist without its own social norms?
- Do you abide by the norms of your own society?
- Do you think that your norms are the norms of others?
- Do you judge others based on your or their norms?
- Would you judge others without knowing their norms?

It is almost impossible to have a unified perception of a single "world," as it will always be distorted due to the differences in individuals' perceptions, judgments, experiences, hidden objectives, and/or bias.

It's Not Always What It Seems to Be!

Our stories of the history of our world have been changed, misinterpreted, mistranslated, and often been misunderstood. Modern views of our world account for many things but sometimes ignore some important aspects. In this article, I will be discussing "Mother Earth." I will not discuss why most people are convinced that the earth is round, why many people still think earth is flat, or why it is called earth despite the fact that only 29% of the surface is actually "earth."

This article will discuss how our world is projected on a map. Yes, maps that we commonly see in classrooms, books, navigation systems, Google, and atlases. The findings shall challenge some ideological assumptions and may change the way you see the real world or even your own world. You may innocently think you have acquired the requisite knowledge. But, it is not always what it seems to be!

Let's have a closer look at the world map.

These common maps were developed as navigational tool for sailors by the Flemish geographer and cartographer Gerardus Mercator in 1569. The method used to generate these maps is called a Mercator projection, which became the standard mapping projection and not only for sailors. The map was represented this way to resolve the challenge associated with portraying the actual 3D spherical world on a flat 2D surface. So, what were the consequences of using Mercator projection?

These maps show distorted areas. This distortion made countries below the equator seem smaller than they should be and all the countries north to it larger than they are.

You may want to have another close look at the map to see that it shows:

- Greenland, China, and Africa of about equal land masses. In reality Africa is 14 times and China is 4 times larger than Greenland.

- Europe being larger than South America while in reality it is half of its size.

- Alaska considerably larger than Mexico but it is not.

- America larger than Africa while it is only one-third of its size.

- China substantially smaller than Scandinavia and that is not true.

You may check that out yourself if you would like to. Try solving the Mercator puzzle map that can be accessed via the following link. It is quite insightful, interesting, and illustrative.

https://gmaps-samples.googlecode.com/svn/trunk/poly/puzzledrag.html

One would ask: If the sizes of countries, continents, seas, and oceans are not right, how about their real locations!!? Well, nothing is where you think it is on the map.

Although these maps were very useful for sailors, some social scientists argue that these maps can adversely influence our perception of various nations and other parts of the world, as we unconsciously correlate size and significance and/or power. When some countries are misrepresented by reducing or exaggerating their sizes, this leads to misconceptions about their importance (i.e., bigger = important, wealthy, powerful; smaller = insignificant, poor, weak). Other scientists claim that initial world maps used to be upside down and north used to be south and south used to be north.

I think upside down maps are equally true if you consider that directions— north, south, east, and west – are essentially arbitrary words used to make sense of direction. Whatever reality is, the sense of direction is not significant if you observe earth from space. What you may be using then, as arbitrary words, to indicate directions could be top, bottom, front, back, left, and right. If you would like to see different kind of projections for world maps, visit http://www.jasondavies.com/maps/. I am sure that these superficial maps were made for reasonable objectives, yet they are perceived accurate through the eyes of the ignorant.

Now, how is the above discussion related to our business, personal, emotional and spiritual worlds?

Every world has its own "countries," "continents," "seas," and "oceans," etc. Every person draws their world map using a unique projection technique that is perceived to be logical, practical, or fit-for-purpose. The chances that the generated map of that "world" is misrepresented and the areas are distorted and dislocated are very possible, and the consequences can be very detrimental. You may comprehend this well and observe the potential impact by looking at the distorted human head drawn using two different projection techniques and reflect on what your "world" would look like using various projections. So, please make sure you use the appropriate projection that serves the purpose.

Many scientists, theologians, and philosophers have been struggling and arguing about methodologies to explore and visualize these individual worlds with the intention to understand how they are drawn in the minds and reflected in reality. What we see from these internal worlds are only projections that are reflected by words and actions. Every projection can get even more distorted and influenced by the interpretation of observers. It is almost impossible to have a unified perception of a single "world," as it will always be distorted due to the differences in individuals' perceptions, judgments, knowledge, experiences, hidden objectives, and/or bias.

These individuals unconsciously tend to DISTORT facts contrary to their conventional wisdom and beliefs (i.e., reduce or exaggerate sizes which can lead to misconceptions about their importance), and unfortunately, emphasize information that supports their views, affirming that "It's not always what it seems to be!"

Challenge Yourself

- Have you ever witnessed a situation where it was not as it seemed to be?
- Have you ever been falsely accused?
- Have you ever wrongly accused someone?
- If you are absolutely sure about something, does it mean you are right?

Once one generation is controlled,
the control of subsequent generations
becomes easier.

Brain Hacking

Hacking is usually associated with computers, satellites, communication, security, cyberspace, and many other "systems" including BRAINS. Although the term hacking is commonly associated with cyber-crimes, it refers to capabilities that technology enthusiasts or "hackers" enjoy practicing to modify or extend features of systems beyond their original purposes.

These practices started more than a century ago in 1878, just after the invention of the telephone by Alexander Graham Bell, when a group of teenagers who were running the switchboards got interested in knowing how the system worked and tried to "hack" it rather than make the proper connection and direct calls. In the 1960s, the time when the word "hacker" began being used at MIT, computer hackers were known for their expertise in hardcore programming, altering and extending capabilities of software and hardware. Although the hackers' initial expertise was applied towards making systems work better and/or faster; some devised means and created boxes to illegally hack telephone systems to make free long distance calls. Over time, hackers have exploited security holes in computer systems and developed means and methods to gain unauthorized access and control to

31

local and remote machines. The term hackers then became associated with cybercrimes subsequent to the invention of the term "cyberspace" in the early 1980s.

Although there isn't magical software to absolutely prevent hackers, asset owners try to protect their systems by various hardware and software means in order to minimize penetration and/or attacks. Unfortunately, history proves that all the measures have never been enough to prevent "harm." Even the largest organizations and agencies like banks, government, intelligence, and security entities have been victims of hackers. Scary, isn't it?

Laymen wish that the original intentions remained and all the systems were kept ISOLATED, without being connected to each other (i.e., physical or wireless). They truly realize the value of advancements in information technologies, connections, and speed, but they also recognize that more catastrophes occurred when more systems were interconnected.

When thinking about communication system timelines, one may realize that the most sophisticated and advanced wireless communication means have been there since the beginning of time. The couriers were primitive but were very effective

CONNECTIONS used to convey a message (send a command) and potentially influence or even control (hack) an outcome. These messages did not require physical transport; they could be sent as drawings or paintings, words, smoke signals, signal flags, body gestures, expressions, books, etc. Amazingly enough, the impact of commands on brains were not limited to a timeframe, but continued to be effective through time, with different locations, different cultures, different languages, different ideologies, different BRAINS, etc. They are by far more complex than commands sent through the current digital world means. The advancement in couriers (e.g., telephone, photography, radio, television, internet…) have not changed them but rather added more effectiveness to them. It was only recently that even brains could be physically wired (electrophysiology). One day, our brains may be physically programmed and eventually similar connections may even become wireless.

Reading the above may suggest that the process of hacking brains is much like hacking computers. One would wonder if there is a means to bypass the will and have partial or full control of your brain!!! Another may doubt if you are the person you think you are!!! We may be just actors who believe the "movie" is real while we are just taking a role designated by an author of our actions, "a brain hacker."

The capabilities of controlling brains is proportionally related to the power of and access to controlling sources of information such as media, education, policies, etc. These "authors," who can be religious leaders, scientists, politicians, and economists have similar interests and every one of them articulates and promotes only a version of truth.

The continuous exposure of brains to the stream of information, unfortunately, could unconsciously outline individuals' and societies' boundaries and meanings of dreams, thoughts, insights, and actions.

Although these information streams may be intended to inform and educate, they could potentially be directed to manipulate, condition, and control. This is something that happens to us every day, which may be referred to as mass psychology, social conditioning, mind manipulation, mind control, or brain hacking.

Once one generation is controlled, naturally, the control of subsequent generations becomes easier. The longer a society believes one version of the truth, the harder it becomes to question it, let alone think about changing it, since this version gets molded at the neurological level and people come to believe it as their own. It just becomes part of their DNA, although most of our identity is a product of influence that can be transformed, but only if we want to.

If there isn't "magical software" to absolutely prevent hackers, the best way is to get disconnected, learn the original essence of hacking, and make sure that you do your own BRAIN HACKING. Human beings function better when they are occasionally disconnected. This is exactly why all the great religious traditions choose to reserve a time for prayers, meditations, and supplications, and a time for contemplations and retreat. Even if humans do not choose to disconnect, they will almost be forced to during their sleep every night.

It is not an easy task nor is it comfortable. It may sound silly, but it is possible to "hack" your own brain if you genuinely want to. You still think you can't do it? Take an acting class, and take a role of the person you want to be; this may help! Everyone with an influence can be, to a certain extent, a brain hacker. The only ones capable of hacking their own brains are those who are in full control of their awareness and are decisive. It is those who can be detached from others (frequently disconnect their brains), let go of prejudice, and who can absolutely be FREE.

Challenge Yourself

- Why do companies and politicians advertise if what we see and hear does not affect us?
- Would anyone ever be able to know that they are brain-hacked?
- Do you think that hacked brains can be repaired?
- Do you think that human beings have capacity to reprogram themselves?

Prisons have transformed and evolved by human beings developing their own distinct invisible walls: walls of fear, walls of comfort zones, walls of history, walls of culture, walls of ideologies, walls of egos, walls of habits, walls of instincts, walls of sins and walls of greed.

Prisoners of the Minds

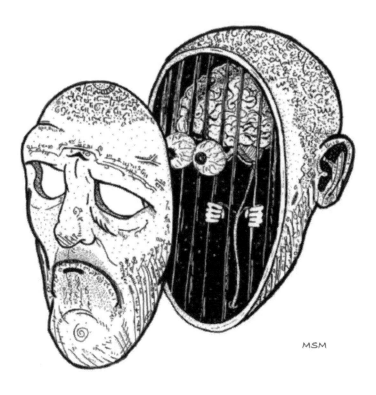

MSM

What goes on in anyone's mind when the word prison is mentioned includes punishment, detention, denial of freedom, and criminal justice, regardless of the type of the prison or the cause of imprisonment. From ancient times, through the Middle Ages and to the modern era, prisons have taken various shapes and forms. From underground dungeons, dark rooms, basements, merchant vessels, or colonies (e.g., Devil's Island) to very advanced technological security confinement cells. From workhouses to work details, from heavy leg irons, chains, and handcuffs, to advanced electronic bracelets and chips.

There are prisons for youth detention, men's, and women's, and prisoners of war, military, political, administrative, psychiatric and even religious. Those prisons are normally surrounded and protected with "walls," guards, and various barriers to prevent escape. Modern prisons are constructed to accommodate hundreds or even thousands of inmates with diversified and sophisticated facilities that differ from one prison to another, from one country to another, depending on culture, funding, etc. A variety of justifications and explanations are put forth for why people are imprisoned. These purposes include retribution, incapacitation, deterrence, and rehabilitation. They are all sought to deter people from committing crime out of fear of going to prison or to instruct prisoners in morality, obedience, and acceptable behavior.

One would argue that it is hard to train for freedom in a prison, and for sure, a man in a prison for part of his life would never fully understand a world outside of that prison, just as people outside prisons would not understand their world!

Some movements and activists seek to reduce or eliminate all sorts of prisons and replace them with more humane systems that add value to "prisoners," their families, societies, and to the whole world. They believe that prisons have not introduced anything good, just suffering and more complications for individuals and societies. With millions people in prisons around the world, governments, technology providers, training program facilitators, and others heavily invest to ensure effective construction and management of these prisons. It is becoming more of an industry, a very big industry! One would guess that these industries would love to turn the whole world into one big prison. Why wouldn't they?

This industry has introduced multiple versions of prisons: Some have people behind bars and others have prisoners behind invisible bars, one subjects inmates to definite sentences and others to an indefinite or a life sentence, some have physical borders and others are borderless, and some have a known population and others have unknown occupants.

An observer sees some societies, academic centers, workplaces, and cultures as different sort of "prisons" and prisoners, prisoners of the mind. We have been doing it this way, living it this way, seeing it this way, and learning it this way, and many have already become "prisoners" and many others have become the guards of these prisons.

When an individual realizes the importance of getting out of the imprisonment or just introducing a change, a combined army of both "external" and "internal" guards tirelessly tries to prevent the individual from changing, advancing, or ever becoming FREE.

They just become scared and resistant to any change. They simply act as though they were "birds born in a cage think flying is an illness." (Alejandro Jodorowski)

It is more of a perception when people view those who oppose the norm from their societies as if they were misfits, trouble makers, or crazy. I very much appreciated the movie "The Truman Show" where **Jim Carrey** became suspicious of his perceived reality and embarked on a quest to discover the truth about his entire life since childhood.

Amazingly, it took him thirty years to discover **by coincidence** that his entire life was only a show, a show reassembled in false reality where he had to secretly search for freedom, overcome fear, and uncover his true identity by exiting through the edge of the dome into the real world. I wonder how many **Jim Carrey's** are living among us and how long it will take them to discover that their lives are only a show!

Prisons have transformed and evolved by human beings developing their own distinct but invisible walls: walls of fear, walls of comfort zones, walls of history, walls of culture, walls of ideologies, walls of habits, walls of egos, walls of instincts, walls of sins, and walls of greed.

When all these irrational invisible walls are used, a human being is highly exploitable, and as such, humans are the most valuable resource, capable of the most extraordinary achievements; as much that they can become the least humane treated unconsciously by oneself or even by loved ones, ironically not by haters or strangers. It is so disappointing and gloomy to accept that people could become **prisoners of the mind,** never realizing that freedom is a state of mind, even when one is behind bars.

Challenge Yourself

- What are your thoughts about conventional prisons?
- What would be alternatives to prisons to achieve the same goals?
- Could a bird learn to fly in a cage/prison?
- Do you feel that you are a prisoner, somehow?
- What would make you feel you are free?

The fact that an individual subconsciously
follows the action of others, is a problem by itself,
irrespective of the actions being right or wrong.

A Society Born with Microtia!

Have you ever seen a child with a small or deformed shaped ear, or even missing an ear? That is known as a Microtia ear. It is a congenital deformity affecting the outer ear where the ear does not fully develop during the first trimester of pregnancy. It commonly occurs with other ear-related defects that commonly happen in one ear, the right ear, with higher occurrences in males. Although there has not been clear evidence on the exact cause of Microtia, various treatments are available.

Microtia occurs in every 1 out of 6,000 to 12,000 births. If it is a rare condition, how would a complete society be born with it?! The following parable will uncover the secret about a Society Born with Microtia.

Once upon a time, there was a King and a Queen who struggled with infertility. The King sought the best doctors from around his kingdom to help his wife become pregnant. God willing, the Queen got pregnant! The King was so happy that he was counting days and nights waiting for the crown prince to come. Nine months passed so slowly... Eventually, the Queen gave birth to a very precious baby boy, the new royal baby, with the King by her side. The same incredibly special and happy moment turned into sadness when the King and his Queen realized that the boy was born with only one ear (i.e., Microtia ear). The public was excitedly awaiting its first glimpse of the little prince and his delighted parents, who were expected to proudly introduce him to the kingdom. The King was more concerned about the future of his son and his feelings. He called upon his ministers and advisors seeking their wisdom. "It is very simple Oh, King; let's cut an ear off every newborn baby" one of his advisors said. The King was impressed by the idea and subsequently, it became the norm in the kingdom to cut an ear off from every newborn. Several decades passed with everyone in the society having only one ear and everyone thought that it was the norm.

One day, when a young man from a neighboring region was crossing the kingdom looking for a job. People were stunned when they saw his two ears and immediately started making fun of him and his two ears. "The man with two ears" they were harassing him. The young man got really annoyed, insecure, disturbed, and confused because he looked different! Unfortunately, the young man precipitously decided to cut his right ear off to become like them. He couldn't handle being rejected or looked at as the odd one in a crowd. The story is especially interesting as it is a prevalent descriptor of a common human behavior: herd behavior. Ironically, the word herd typically defines or describes a group of animals of the same species that live and move together, either wild or domestic, like sheep or whales. It is just patronizing for human intellects to act like members of herds.

Examples of the herd behaviors include stock market trends, superstition, smart phones, social media, haircuts/styles, etc. Apparently, we can be influenced easily by people around us even if we believe that our choices are purely our own best judgments, without even realizing it. The fact that an individual subconsciously follows the action of others is a problem by itself irrespective of the actions being right or wrong.

SSM

Those individuals "have hearts with which they do not comprehend, they have sight but no vision, and they have ears with which they do not hear." I wish the "ear" were a physical ear and all you would need is a normal mirror. :)

Respected readers, you need to have an "internal mirror" that reflects who you genuinely are, whether you are a member of "A Society Born with Microtia" or not.

Now, are you really free, and are the choices that you are making your own choices? Are you conscious of how other people around you are likely to influence your choices? Are you allowing others to tell you how you should think, feel, or behave?

Take your time and make a conscious effort to form your own opinions, be aware of the decisions you make and their consequences, and be brave and free enough to stand out and be the odd one in the crowd, even if you are the only one with two ears in "A Society Born with Microtia."

Challenge Yourself

- It is hard to imagine that you can be one of those with one ear? :) How would you know if this is the case?

- Do you question the accepted paradigms of the society, at least inwardly, when challenging these paradigms externally is forbidden or unwise?

- Would you accept Microtia when it is expedient?

Only those who earn power will be able
to give it away and amazingly enough,
become more powerful.

When Leaders Walk Naked

This is a multi-purpose short post: to test, to "expose," to entertain, and to hopefully enlighten.

If you get offended by 18+ (adult) content, close your eyes or just stop here!

If you dislike observing people "stripped," stop here!

If you want to laugh and learn and don't mind 18+ content, read the rest of this post.

The word naked has multiple meanings and uses. The word has various connotations that evoke positive or negative feelings and reactions. There's an interesting irony about how the connotations evolve with time; this word has totally changed connotations! The word naked has the same technical definition of being exposed, vulnerable, embarrassing, or uncovered for things that are normally concealed. It may also be used with less negative or acceptable connotations such as "bare": naked eye, naked truth, naked wire, and naked to one's enemies.

The word naked has a unique influence, flavor, and magic lure whether perceived as positive or a negative word.

The influence of the title of this post can be measured by the number of its readers. I wonder if my intuition is right and the number of readers for this article will exceed that of other articles in the book! The statistics of shown in the below art may demonstrate my message. I may be wrong though, thinking that text is not as appealing as photographs.

Isn't it exactly the same strategy used in other media channels, be it visual, oral, or written? Whether you see it as right or wrong is immaterial. It is the way it is. All you can do is to make sure your contribution to Media-Universe is decent, of value, something you would treasure forever and will never make you feel "naked."

Prior to writing this article, I got curious about the combination of two words and how they are associated: Naked and Leaders. When I searched for the combination of the words "naked" and "leaders," I found a book titled *The Naked Leader* by David Taylor. This book is a leadership book with some unique perspectives that intend to strip away doubts and uncertainties in an articulated approach which demonstrates to readers that they have what it

53

takes to be successful. Several similar books and articles have been published about naked leaders, naked leadership, getting naked, and others. They all consider the word naked as a positive = transparent with people they serve, etc., as if true leaders need reminders about essential attributes of leadership. True leaders just have them engraved in their personalities and they just spontaneously LEAD. Those who are not true leaders may pretend to be, but their truth will be revealed one day.

Now, it is time for the entertaining part of the article, a short story, a very popular story by Hans Christian Anderson, "The Emperor's New Clothes," which I guess most of the readers know well. But for the sake of those who are unfamiliar with the story, here is its summary.

A couple of tailors come to town and convince the emperor the clothes they weave are of the finest quality but are visible only to those who are truly worthy. The emperor had them make some for him. Even though the emperor realizes he can't see the cloth, neither he nor anyone else dares to say they don't see it and embarrass themselves and the emperor. The emperor proudly walks down the main street in a parade and everyone goes along with the charade. All people pretend not to notice until a young child cries out loud: "How could the emperor be so crazy to walk naked?" Shamefully enough, the parade continues as if the emperor's "illusion" is a reality and as if the masks worn by everyone else are the true faces (other than the child who wears no mask). The story is available online in various forms and lengths and from various cultures at various times.

Self-deception is the modern version of this story, and it happens too often for political, organizational, social, and theological leaders. The emperor resembles a leader, the tailors resemble consultants, the cloth resembles a project, people are team members/workers/followers, and the young child represents those who are honest.

Doesn't it sound so very familiar?

Some leaders are just like the emperor wearing an invisible suit, conducting projects for the higher purpose of their organizations and themselves. They march and get the support of all the subordinates who fear being "odd" and choose to be "yes-people" or the least to be silent. Although, a "child" may declare the truth about the project by stating it is a failure, everyone else pretends not to notice. Time flies and the investment become so huge (more of snowball effect) that it becomes a matter of pride or acceptable norm, and this is when leaders will shamefully continue to walk naked. What is worse than being naked in front of other is the denial that one may have of being naked even when standing in front of a mirror.

One would wish that organizations are led by that "young child" or maybe have him at least as an advisor to the emperor.

I am very confident that you have witnessed at least one version of a similar story during your lifetime, if you are 18+. You could have been the emperor, one of the tailors, one of the truly worthy, one of the normal people, or the young child.

Challenge Yourself:

- Have you witnessed such a case and what was your role and what did you do about it?
- "Unlimited power is apt to corrupt the minds of those who possess it." Is this true?
- What would you do if you had absolute power?
- Will you choose to be the "young child?"

Science will never be able to comprehend, prove or disprove anything beyond the circle of knowledge because it is taking its data from within the circle itself.

Gravity – The Mysterious Force!

Gravity is among those wonders that we profoundly believe in, yet no one knows what this force really is. It is among numerous things that we have not touched, seen, smelled, heard, or even tasted. Although it plays a significant role in our universe, most people do not even think about it. It is among the many "obvious" things we sense, describe, theorize, and talk about as if everyone very well knows all about it. Isn't it true that "everything that goes up must come down" due to a force that we call gravity?

For God sake, it is gravity; don't you know what gravity is?

I really do not know what gravity is. I tell you what: Even physicists, cosmologists, and theologians, who think about such all the time, do not. This topic is among the most controversial subjects among scientists and theologians. To them, gravity is still a mystery with potential implications of uncovering how the universe works, yet all we can say is that this mystery has gotten deeper. Even at this moment, no one is entirely sure what gravity is or where it comes from!

So, what was the start? Was it Newton's theory of the falling apple in 1666? For an observer, Newton's theory violates the physical laws about forces. According to Newton's law of motion, "for every action or force there is an equal yet opposite reaction," except for gravity. Gravity is always a pulling and attracting force! One may argue that even electromagnetic force pulls. Yes, it does, but it can also repel based on the charges of the bodies within a system. Scientists go around this by making gravity a property of the fabric of the universe, not of individual bodies, as Einstein proposed in 1915, or by associating it with an imaginary repulsing form of gravitational force that is associated with "Dark Energy." Well, no one knows what this dark energy is, and to many, they are imaginative ideas or science fiction stories. It seems that all the methods of science can produce are empirical theories that are based on assumptions, with some of these theories, unfortunately, becoming dogmas.

If none of the theories cover all aspects of gravity and with all the discrepancies among the various theories, one could rightly presume that there could be a glitch in how we understand the quantum theory of sub-atomic structures and cosmic universes, assuming the absence of a "unifying theory" of physics or simply:

We don't know what we don't know. Although many scientists have long claimed comprehension of all of the gravitational forces, a layman may still have doubt about the accuracy of these theories. Many scientists believe that the understanding of the universe and the existence will not be completed until the secrets about gravity are uncovered. You never know what this understanding may bring; it may lead to attaining the capabilities to manipulate gravity, invent anti-gravity gizmos, or it may lead to venues for surprising knowledge, even beyond the realms of science fiction.

It would be fascinating to know what could happen if gravity were switched off, wouldn't it? Well, based on the available mathematical predication capabilities, time and space will disappear upon the disappearance of gravity. One can rightly refer to scriptures about how easily a camel could go through the eye of a needle. I wonder if the same thing could apply to earth or to the whole universe. Science will never be able to comprehend, prove, or disprove anything beyond the circle of knowledge because it is taking its data from within the circle itself.

Isn't it a mind-boggling scenario to imagine how galaxies, stars, planets, and life have formed if the expansion force of universe continuously overwhelms gravitational forces? It is equally a mind-boggling scenario to imagine that gravitational forces are stronger! If any of these scenarios took place, there would be nothing left to call a universe. We are very blessed with regulated forces since the birth of the universe or by a universe of total energy equals zero, resulting theoretically in an everlasting universe.

During a family visit to the Florida Keys, we stopped by the Coral Castle (claiming to be the 8th wonder of the modern world) in Homestead City, just south of Miami. The currently known Coral Castle was originally named "Rock Gate Park" and was built during the years 1923-51 by Edward Leedskalnin – one man, ~5 feet tall and barely 100 pounds. Ed quarried and moved about 1,000 tons of heavy pieces of coral from the earth with the heaviest weighing over 28 tons and erected them by himself using primitive tools. Some people think that he was able to reduce or even eliminate the earth's gravitational force (i.e., capitalized on anti-gravity technologies). "I have discovered the secrets of the pyramids, and have found out how the Egyptians and the ancient builders in Peru, Yucatan, and Asia, with only primitive tools, raised and set in place blocks of stone weighing many tons!" Edward said. Others have suggested that "the story of the Coral Castle has intrigued people and has attracted tourists from around the world, yet it is a myth and the truth is less intriguing."

The notion of constructing anti-gravity technologies has been a dream for many throughout history. No one has done it. An observer may ask: Why does anyone presume it is even possible? Invisible gravitational forces have been attracting different masses in the universe to each other. These masses have different sizes, colors, shapes and locations, yet they attract each other. It looks like gravity among humans is a bit different from that of planets. People get mostly attracted or attached to those who look like them, who share common ideas, values, and interests, etc., and almost always, are not attracted to those who are different.

One thing to remember is the attracting invisible force that we call gravity is the thing that keeps US standing firmly on the earth and, with no pillars, holds the entire universe together. Imagine the universe and earth with no gravity!

The Law of Universal Gravitation shows that gravity is proportional to the masses, and inversely proportional to the square of the distance between two objects. An observer would wish that the law of human relationships might resemble Newton's, a law that does not discriminate between colors, shapes or composition but is affected only by the size and proximity of objects. This human gravitational force would be magnified when they do not only become "closer" but also when they have bigger "masses" (i.e. minds, souls, spirits and hearts) irrespective of ideologies, cultures, heritages, colors, and genders.

It is that gravitational force that is associated with minds, souls, spirits, hearts, and bodies. These invisible forces are the mystical "human gravitational force" that mirrors righteous attributes, feelings, thoughts, and intentions including love, hope, compassion, happiness, forgiveness, generosity, kindness, gratitude, and peacefulness. These gravitational forces are the things that shall keep us standing firmly on earth. Imagine humans without this sort of "gravity"!

Challenge Yourself:

- How many obvious things you don't comprehend well other than gravity?
- Do you believe that science will one day explain everything?
- What is it that attracts you to others and how is this attraction measured?

Genuine leaders are the drivers for continuous
progress and the creators of corporate culture of
stronger architecture,
a culture that can create a suitable environment
conducive for highly motivated professionals
to be proactive, efficient, healthy, and fulfilled.

Who Dares to Grab a Banana?

Human culture is "the knowledge" of a specific group or society, a social heritage that encompasses knowledge, values, ideas, assumptions, language, beliefs, and artifacts as well as behaviors, customs, and cuisine. Ironically, the process for passing cultural perceptions from one generation to another is the same for both moral and immoral values, as if different cultures have common perception about moral values. These perceptions are often passed without being examined or thoroughly thought out. Generations might willingly accept them and continue to implement them and never question the wisdom behind doing that.

The same consequences occur by other causes such as contentment, preconceived notions, ignorance, lack of insight, myths, **FEAR** or **INTIMIDATION**. The latter two are very well related, and they are the subject of this article, which starts with a famous story about the five monkeys experiment.

The experiment began with a group of scientists placing five monkeys in a cage, and in the middle, a ladder with bananas on top. As soon as one of the monkeys started to climb the ladder, all monkeys were soaked with ice cold water. Then, every time a monkey went up the ladder, the scientists soaked the rest of the monkeys with ice cold water. After some time, every time a monkey would start climbing up the ladder, the others would pull it down and beat it up. The scientists shut off the ice cold water source and observed that no monkey would dare to climb the ladder.

Then, the scientists decided to replace one of the five monkeys with a new monkey. The first thing the new monkey did was to climb the ladder. Immediately, the others four monkeys pulled him down and beat him up. After several beatings, the new monkey learned to never go up the ladder, even though there was no obvious reason not to, aside from the beating. A second monkey out of the remaining four was replaced and the same thing occurred. Ironically, the first monkey participated in the beating of the second monkey. The same story occurred when the rest of the three monkeys were replaced. At the end, what was left in the cage were the five new monkeys that did not experience the ice cold water, but continued to beat up any monkey "**WHO DARED TO GRAB A BANANA.**" If they were asked, "why not?" they would simply say, "as far as we know, it has always been done this way."

Whether the experiment is true or not should not make any difference. The monkeys' brains formed an association between the attempt to climb (achieve) and the cold ice water (intimidation), and seeing any monkey trying to climb elicited an alarm for other monkeys in preparation to attack. One may say that fear helps mankind to cope with challenges in life. This is somehow true, and let's call it a healthy fear. But when fear interferes with the ability to live and thrive, it becomes a great problem, especially when it evolves to become a hard-wired attribute. This counterproductive attribute can result by practices of some self-centered leaders/managers that only care about their own benefits, even if it is at the expense of the organization. These are the types of leaders who Manage By Intimidation (MBI).

Again, these lessons learned can be associated with all industries, countries, religions, cultures, and societies. The focus in this article will again be more on business culture transformation where a change management's contribution is significant in supporting the "corporate culture" that is supposed to be free of MBI. Genuine leaders are the drivers for continuous progress and the creators of corporate culture with stronger architecture, a culture that can create a suitable environment conducive for highly motivated professionals to be proactive, efficient, healthy, and fulfilled. This culture would have the potential to join the fittest and could be among the last ones standing in an ever-increasing competitive business. To have such a culture, we may need to have all of the "monkeys" replaced at the same time and that is not actually feasible, in reality.

For this to happen, leaders must eradicate consequences of MBI by articulating and implementing the prerequisites to achieve corporate short- and long-term objectives. This is done to establish a constitution with corporate governance which ensures autonomy, continuity, and alignment.

We need to ask ourselves if we have inherited any MBI practices, if we probably contribute to it, or if we can help the monkey "who dares to grab a banana."

Challenge Yourself:

- Have you ever accepted to continue with a cultural practice that you are not convinced of, without questioning the wisdom behind it?
- How often you hear this term: "it has always been done this way"?
- Who should lead cultural change in a rapidly changing world?

Culture's endless and evolutionary journey
plays a major role in shaping the way of our lives
and the lives of the generations to come.

Where is the Rest of my Fish?

MSM

Culture influence is manifested on society members' responses and the interactions among each other and their surroundings. These responses or practices are perceived to be legitimate, acceptable and correct, and will find their way to be passed on to the new members through communication, imitation, teaching, and learning.

Culture's endless and evolutionary journey plays a major role in shaping the ways of our lives and the lives of generations to come. In the previous article, you have observed how social norms have formed as consequences of fear and intimidation. Similar consequences could occur due to either ignorance, lack of insight or knowledge. How does this happen? The following funny parable will make you cr-augh (i.e. cry and laugh) as it relates to many perceptions we have towards various things.

Once upon a time, a man who had some trouble with his wife because she brought him his fried fish without its tail and head.

"Darling, **where is the rest of my fish?** They are my favorite parts" the husband asked.

"I threw them away" the wife said.

"Why did you do that?" He asked.

"Well, I saw my Mom doing it so", she explained.

"But, why did she do so? Darling", he asked

"I don't know", the wife said

The couple decided to visit with the Mom to ask her why she was throwing the head and the tail. When they asked her, she did not know either and all she said was that she learned it from her Mom. Fortunately, the grandma was alive so they paid the old lady a visit to uncover the secret. When they told her the story, she laughed a lot and revealed the secret.

"Once upon a time, your grandpa brought a fish, a big fish, and all we had was too small frying pan and I had to cut the head and the tail to fry the fish," the grandma said. Literature has many similar stories.

They all confirm that (1) misconceptions affect the way we process information leading to potentially devastating results. In this case, we ended up with two generations wasting "delicious heads and tails of fish," (2) old habits die hard; and (3) challenging conventional wisdom has to be considered a virtue.

The story encourage us to "challenge paradigms and to make an impact" and not to accept that "we have always done it that way" as our only way of life. These tips fit many situations in our life and can have a great influence on the success or failure of journeys, relations, projects and endeavors.

Challenge Yourself:

- Have you ever wanted to see how others perceive your cultural values?
- Have you mentally or emotionally rejected any cultural value but kept practicing it?
- Have you ever succeeded to change your comfort zone?

Theoretical approaches and conceptual designs of solutions can be described, articulated, and presented; they work very well
in PowerPoint slides, don't they? However, applying many of them remains easier said than done, as many are finding

When Sheep Beat Tigers

Once upon a time, technology experts, scientists and inventors gathered to discuss the imperatives that are crucial to the success of their technical projects, transformation programs and human resources. They have identified many challenges including technological, logistical, cultural and personal. They were determined to bring about a revolutionary solution to attain significant success and growth in their programs. They elected to start their mission by focusing on technologies.

Many examples were given to demonstrate the evolution of various technologies and their impact on performance, business environment, advancement and profit. Many innovators and entrepreneurs, among the participants, have demonstrated great ideas about some disruptive technologies and programs that are conceptually fascinating, yet their tangible values aren't seen until after "years" of Research and Development, trial tests, implementation and hopefully utilization.

All industries strive to meet their own objectives and they do not invest in any technology for the sake of it. They are not a bunch of

Luddites. Some companies target, invest, and pilot certain technologies and business models even if they have not matured yet. Whatever the justification is for these technologies (e.g., economical, strategic), they trust that piloting such technologies provides unique learning opportunities and insights into their effectiveness and applications; hence, it facilitates good results sooner, as well as learning and benefits.

I am sure many visionaries prepare for unintended consequences that might lead to a discovery of new ideas or may lead to undesirable risks or complexities. Despite the growing importance of various technologies in our life, many technological projects fail miserably. Ironically enough, most of these failures are due a non-technical issue including: poorly defined objectives, lack of leadership, lack of accountability, lack of transparency and communication or lack of a clear plan. Apart of the technical contents of the discussion, a strange question was raised by the youngest audience. It was about sheep and tigers.

Question: Which one of the two species will have a higher population increase rate, assuming no external factors exist?

He has offered the audience more facts about sheep and tigers shown below.

The audience did not have to think much about it to give their answers. It must be tigers as demonstrated in the below chart.

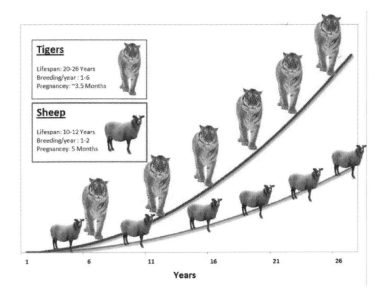

My dear reader, in reality there are more "weak" sheep than "strong" tigers. In fact, a hundred years ago, there were more than 100,000 tigers, but today we have only ~ 3000 tigers; they are becoming extinct. On the other hand, the sheep population is still growing – do you know that there are more sheep in Australia than its population?

It is not the physical fitness (~ money); nor is it the rate of reproduction (~ implementations). It must be something else!

The intent again was to emphasize one of the most important attributes one may have towards a project, any project. It is about an attribute that grant projects more improvement, higher growth and significant success opportunities. "What is that thing?" the young man asked.

Well, sheep have owners who provide continuous and unconditional care. The above questions were just "tips" to demonstrate the significant role of the sense of ownership, knowledge, care and clarity of vision and objectives. Without these attributes, any personal or professional project is prone to definite failure.

No doubt, business value has already resulted from many technology implementations, but there are still more opportunities to be captured and many lessons to be learned to take full advantage of the investments. Continued improvisation of implementation methods can result in the perception that the industries are just very uncertain and wasteful to warrant significant time, attention, and resources.

Theoretical approaches and conceptual designs of solutions can be described, articulated, and presented; they work very well in PowerPoint slides, don't they? However, applying many of them remains easier said than done as many are finding out. Although, the discussion above is mostly about technologies and reasons why they either fail or succeed, the same is very applicable to any project in our lives. This can be a project for you, your family, society, nation and even the entire earth. I am sure by now; you know how sheep beat the tigers.

Challenge Yourself:

- What is it that you consider the most important project of your life?
- Have you been giving it enough care?
- What would be your success criteria?

Close your "real eyes" for a moment
and think about how much clutter
you have collected in your mind.
You may need to do some housekeeping.

Blinking Minds

Blinking Minds!!! What an unusual title. A common use of the word "blinking" is always associated with optics (eyes, stars, LEDs, flashing lights, etc.). It all boils down to the power of vision, a precious gift that we might only appreciate enough if we could see through the eyes of a blind man, whose physical world is black forever.

If one assumes that an adult blinks an average of 20 blinks a minute with a blink speed of one-tenth of a second, one would have his/her eyes closed about ~4% of their waking time. Every time one blinks, the eyelids equally spread a film of tears across the surface of the eyes to keep them safe, moist, and clean. You may be wondering why you don't feel the world plunging into darkness every time you blink!! You are probably thinking about it now.

Those quick moments of "darkness," the blinks, with a tears-drain system are very essential to the health of eyes. With greater knowledge about these systems and their functionalities, one could pause and acknowledge their significance.

There are things we take for granted, not realizing that someone else is praying for, so always be grateful for all that you have. In this context: a healthy eye, healthy tear glands, and a healthy drainage system.

The consequences can be very severe if any of these systems are not functioning properly. You do not want to see an eye with a blocked tear duct.

What is fascinating about blinking is the fact that it is a protective reflex and happens so fast that no one notices it nor does anyone even think about it. In fact, the human brain tends to ignore this momentary "blackout." Some scientists claim that the act of blinking overwhelms the activities in several areas of the brain to a degree; it makes them experience the world as continuous. Other scientists suggest that the act of blinking not only refreshes and protects the eyes but also provides the brain with a break that facilitates more focus and greater attention. No wonder some people close their eyes when they want to give more focus or deeply think. It is incredible to realize how we picture reality, imagine images, and frame beliefs while our eyes are closed. It is the ability of the mind's eye to perceive the sensible world and beyond. The mind's eye sees things based on interpretation of the input data from all of the senses and within imagination limits. Internal eyes struggle to interpret optical illusion images as still images. The only time you see it still is the first glance with no focus. Amazing, eh! Maybe sometimes we need to not focus to see reality!

What may sound surprising is the observation that MRI images of the brain of a person seeing, thinking, or imagining an event; all the MRI images look identical. The brain doesn't differentiate whether these images were seen by the real or mind's eye. Whatever the images are, they will bring about similar feelings, positive or negative, to the extent that some imaginations produce some symptoms of real illnesses manifested as happiness or even rashes and bruises on the skin. One can't imagine how empty the world would be if our mind's eyes were blind even for a short while. The world you see is an image as seen by your mind's eye.

One can decide to stop blinking an eye, maybe for few seconds or so, but then the automatic control comes in to take charge. There is only one safe and effective way to stop blinking: close your eyes and meditate, or take the easiest approach – go to sleep. During these times, your eyelids do not blink, but some other eyes start blinking: your internal eyes, the blinking mind.

You might wish your mind would blink more frequently while you are awake. If a healthy physical eye helps you see and recognize your loved ones, appreciate nature, recognize other creatures, and differentiate between shapes, sizes, and colors, an internal healthy eye should help you travel to the past, value the presence, see the future, and face the unknown. When we have the courage to face the unknown, we can examine new ideas, challenge conventional wisdom, go to places we never expected to go, or develop a relationship with different people, or just be someone who is not a clone or an imitator of others. Life is sometimes filled with twists, turns, desires, responsibilities, challenges, disputes, differences, and uncertainties, etc. The blinking of the mind can be a process to relieve stress and explore better opportunities. A blinking mind will yield a clear vision, stable emotions, a healthier heart, an enlightened spirit, and a free soul. Close your "real eyes" for a moment and think about how much clutter you have collected in your mind. You may need to do some housekeeping. :)

Some of this clutter is stuff (e.g., regrets, unfinished tasks, conflicts, worries, etc.) that you need to dispose of, and then replace with better things. Just allow your mind to blink. Wish it were a reflex with tears-film to keep the mind "safe," "moist," and "clean," and wish it had an effective duct system to drain pride, immorality, and greed.

Challenge Yourself:

- What feelings come to you when you remember or imagine good or bad incidents?
- Do you realize that how you feel is influenced by what you see through your mind's eye?
- Have you ever reacted to situations based on only feelings?

If you consider the Devil the enemy,
there may be more to learn from your enemy
than from many of your friends.

Let's Learn from the Devil

I believe that you may feel as though the title is sacrilegious. However, it's not what it sounds like. If you consider the Devil the enemy, there may be more to learn from your enemy than from many of your friends. This is beyond all Godly lessons learned. It brings you to a mental state that leads you to look for the goodness in others, even if you think they are bad.

Back to my subject – let's learn from the Devil: The first sin the Devil committed was disobeying God. Why? He just thought he was better. It's arrogance that got him kicked out of Heaven. Those who are Devil-like, think they're better and may act as if they're GODS. We should not let arrogance (I am better, I know more!) take control over our views, life, career, and decisions. It is just a trap. So, what can we learn from the Devil?

The "Three Ps" stand as clear attributes of the Devil. They are Passion, Patience, and Perseverance. These three Ps, if harnessed, are most often associated with success.

The destruction, terror, suffering, and pain that the world has witnessed and is still witnessing are all confirmations of how devils and their servants religiously practice these three Ps in any of their missions. One would wish that everyone had similar attributes about their own missions, hopefully good missions.

Ironically, some religious and political leaders display many of these qualities; they are arrogant, self-centered, and are strong in the three Ps. An observer would feel very suspicious about the motivations of these leaders and realize that the Devil is very much not alone in this world. One of the biggest, most wicked attributes of the Devil's is arrogance, a disease that could not kill them once but will in the future.

Passion provides continuous momentum and drive to move forward or a catalyst to speed up a process. The Devil is very passionate about his mission and extremely focused on achieving his desired goals. Be passionate about your mission. "One person with passion is better than forty people merely interested." E. M. Forster

Patience is always associated with hard work, commitment, and dedication. Patience is one of the important attributes of leaders as it is seen as a capacity and tolerance to face hardship and inconvenience. The Devil is so patient and sees no obstacle that cannot be overcome with strategic and consistent plans. :)

Believe that "Patience is a Virtue." Only those who have the patience to do simple things perfectly will acquire the skill to do difficult things easily.

Perseverance is always associated with persistence, continuity, and focus. In life, many impaired people show perseverance and keep pursuing their chosen path despite disabilities and difficulties. Many don't give up and even if they fail, they will not say "I have failed many times" but instead say "I have tried several times and I will continue trying." They remain focused and keep motivated, always finish what they start and never, ever give up.

Remain blessed.

Challenge Yourself:

- Do you see good attributes in your enemy?
- Have you ever perceived yourself as your own enemy?

Those who believe in the positive power of words recognize that being speechless makes them powerless, and they believe words are mightier than bullets, spears, and swords.

An Army of Words

The history of human languages and their origin is a fascinating subject and continues to be a subject of research, dispute, and obscurity. The available historical knowledge is insufficient to explain not only how speech was developed, but also why different languages exist. Among the thousands of languages and among the millions of words spoken today, no one knows what the first language was nor does anyone know what the first word was. Historians, philosophers, religious people, and researchers have various views about when and where language(s) originated or were created, or how they evolved. Regardless of what the actual truth about the origin of language is, it is quintessentially a human trait.

There were several attempts to identify the linguistic relationship between words and swords and how they were derived. Whatever the relationship is, both can have mutual connotations, similar uses, and effects. Based on their context, they give us the symbolism for wisdom, duality, strength, power, energy, protection, unity, aggression, destruction, construction, courage, leadership, love, hate, etc.

One would wish they could always be used wisely, peacefully, and constructively. In certain ways, words can heal and in other ways, they can hurt. People frequently underestimate the pain a single word could cause to others. What may have no effect on one person may hurt another, and what may hurt someone could destroy another. Positive, peaceful, and kind words will never cause damage. Would they?

Although words represent the basic element of a language, they harness power, magic, and energy beyond what one can imagine. The energy within words was a subject of a *New York Times* bestseller book, *The Hidden Messages of Water*, which was written by the Japanese author, Masaru Emoto, and subsequently translated into twenty-four languages. Emoto claims that human consciousness and thoughts have an effect on the molecular structure of water, which was visually captured at the moment of freezing as water crystals.

We know that 79% of the earth is made of water, 60% of the human body is made of water, and everything we eat contains water (e.g., 96% of a cucumber). One should definitely be concerned about the water in our bodies and how the energy within words can influence it and hence, influence not only us but also everything around us, if the author's claim is correct. Whether we know or do not know how words influence our bodies, we may predict that one day we will consciously be able to control and influence our bodies.

If just one or a few word(s) can have an impact, one would wonder what a stream or an army of words would do, whatever the source of this stream of words is: writing, printing, radio, TV, social media, or even those words that are invisible (e.g., insinuation, gestures, images etc.). Social media has great effects on individuals and societies. They influence, create values, and introduce different norms. Social media has a power to not only change individuals or societies but to change the entire world. Reality shows that no one can defeat the impact of words with physical powers. Words, propaganda, media, books, revelations or even taking the rational approach have always been the backbone of historical revolutions and transformations, and always will be.

People follow dreams (words) or theocratic-religious beliefs to find happiness and thus support their own points of view, misconceptions, historical fallacies, or causes. However, words can also reveal the truth that inspires, encourages, and teaches; they can show compassion, care, passion, and love.

A reasonable question would be: who controls this power and what is it for? The irony is that the contents of all social media are merely products of the same individuals and/or societies. They usually possess limited knowledge and/or are themselves influenced by "mainstream media," which is employed or susceptible to propaganda, bias and unfairness, to say the least. So, beware of those who claim to know the truth; listen only to those who claim to be seeking the truth.

The journey to truth is not an easy one; it may be tiring, scary, long, painful, and undoubtedly endless. During this journey, one would need a very wise, patient, responsible, resilient, caring, and peaceful "army"; the best of all would be "an army of words." Those who believe in the positive power of words recognize that being speechless makes them powerless, and they believe that words really are mightier than bullets, spears, and swords.

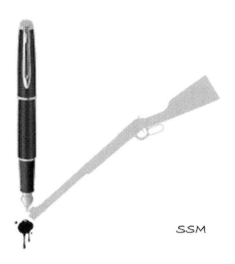

SSM

Challenge Yourself:

- What has greater impact: "words" or "swords"?

- Are you still hurt by a word that hurt you long ago?

- Would you reassess the way you select your words based on the above?

- Would you elect to be speechless if you see injustice done?

- What are the most influential words that have changed your life?

If you accept that zero is everything and at the same time it is nothing,
then it is possible that the creation was initiated from "nothing" and so will it end.

Zero: The Infinity's Twin!

Misrepresentations that are based on inadequate or incomplete data lead to the evolution of misconceptions or myths. These misconceptions or myths, by virtue of their existence can attain the status of truth, acceptable and unchallenged truth. Perceptions vary but can also oppose what is perceived as insignificant to some, yet might be extremely significant to others. So, how is that related to zero, the subject of this article?

Zero, the significant/insignificant number, took centuries to develop, many nations to cross, and great minds to comprehend. Some civilizations chose to live without zero, and they functioned perfectly well. Zero was not significant to Greeks or geometry. The significance of zero materialized only in recent times, and even more in today's connected world where zero plays major roles in such areas as calculus, accounting, computing, etc. Just imagine what your feeling would be like if a zero were erased or added to your monthly pay check, not to the left of the number but to the right. :)

Charles Seife said "Zero is so powerful that it is considered infinity's twin. They are equal and opposite. The biggest questions in science and religion are about nothingness and eternity, the void and the infinite, zero and infinity." When some consider zero as "nothing," others consider it as "everything." How is that possible?

If we take all the numbers (1 plus -1, 2 plus -2, 3 plus -3, 4 plus -4...) that are equal (0 + 0 + 0 + 0...) to zero; this zero is not a "nothing," but instead it can be considered as the largest value in the mathematical system, which also includes the two infinities. If this is considered true, then all other numbers have a lesser value than that of the whole of zero, but still, both positive and negative will be huge.

Saying $0 - (-5) = 5$ makes perfect sense in ordinary math; however, putting out this idea of zero being all numbers and all other numbers being slightly less than zero that requires a paradigm shift. This shift takes us to an understanding that the broken symmetry which creates our universe or any other can be defined by what's missing from it. In the case of our own universe, scientists believe there is much less antimatter than would be expected if our universe were derived from an underlying symmetric state. The absence of antimatter; however, remains a big mystery yet to be resolved by modern physics, with many scientists considering antimatter as a science fact, not fiction.

If you accept that zero is everything and at the same time it is nothing, then it is possible that the creation was initiated from nothing, and so will it end.

The intention of the above discussion is not to dive into physics, mathematics, or religion; rather, it's to point out a few astonishing thoughts to stimulate and intrigue readers.

It is fair to say that prior knowledge and interests of readers and/or writers determine how much they comprehend and how well they can communicate about a certain topic. However, in our universe, around us and within us, many questions remain unanswered, many mysteries remain unresolved, and many phenomena remain unexplained or beyond comprehension. Light, shadow, time, gravity, taste, emotions, pain, consciousness, and knowledge are various forms of energy that are hard to define or weigh. Although man invented means and methods to measure time and gravity, etc., man is still unable to define what they really are. To me, knowledge remains a fascinating subject that researchers and scientists have been investing extensive efforts to define, to streamline and to preserve. If knowledge, ideas or virtues are considered forms of weightless energy (i.e., you don't weigh more if you know more), then the law of conservation of energy states that the total energy of an isolated system remains constant. Energy can be neither created nor destroyed, but it can change forms. To explore readers' approaches and thoughts to preserve this sort of energy (i.e., knowledge), I would love to see a means to preserve knowledge, particularly tacit knowledge, love, wisdom, and understanding. Hopefully, the ideas in this article and the discussions can result in some constructive thoughts. It is only when you know more, you realize that all we know is infinitesimal (i.e. zero) if compared to infinity.

Challenge Yourself:

- How do you formulate your perceptions?
- Do you think it is fair to pass judgments based on perceptions?
- How do you define the significance of things?

As much as it may be comforting to know that good can come from bad circumstances, it is disturbing to know that bad things can come from good circumstances.

What if I Saw Tomorrow!

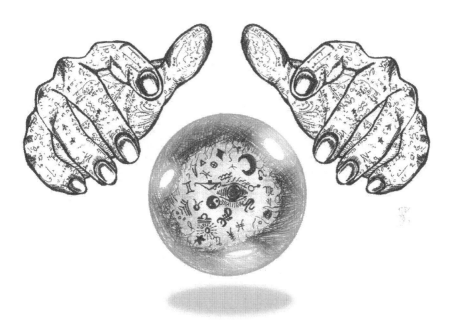

Wouldn't it be fun to know what comes next?

I am sure it would be a great fun to those who work in the stock market. :)

"It could be perceived as a blessing when all that future is bringing is good news! This will make me miss some surprises in life but can also help me avoid some pitfalls," one says. Another one may perceive seeing the future as a curse, especially if all that the future brings are unavoidable catastrophes that cannot be avoided.

It is just hard to comprehend how any person creates a unique mental reality out of his or her own perception of thoughts, images, imaginations, or "prophecies." These mental realities can mysteriously influence personalities, beliefs, and behaviors. Everyone has a mental reality that is influenced by a unique history, present, or future. If this is the case, then reality must be different from those thoughts in our minds.

One would argue how could future events that do not exist and haven't yet occurred have an influence on the human mind? One possible reason is that all future events, even if they haven't occurred in life, were made by or happened in someone's mind, irrelevant of time.

This subject is very debatable yet interesting to study and discuss, and it could have some consensus rather than just arguments. The knowledge about the future is similar to that of death and the afterlife, which remains a debatable subject among psychics, fortune tellers, philosophers, theologians, and scientists. None of them can claim to be an expert on the future, for there is nothing to know about it and no one has travelled into the future and come back. Regardless of what might happen in the future, assume that you could see it and would like to change it. The least this would require is to change your present and the perception and influence of the past that brought you to where you are now. It is just like an endless process, isn't it? It looks like that the only thing that hopefully we have the maximum control of is only one moment, the present moment.

If one considers the universe follows the cause and effect law which states that every cause has an effect and every effect becomes the cause of something else. Then, watch it and be careful when you do anything, literally anything, even if you think it is insignificant; it does affect you and what affects YOU could affect everything around you.

Now, let's see the future through different eyes, an eye that sees the best is yet to come and another one that sees the worst is yet to come.

One sees an imminent collapse of the physical, spiritual, social, financial, and emotional world, while the other sees that the world is going through a temporary "pregnancy pain" represented by all the existing challenges and suffering that will eventually end up with a birth – a birth of the truth that should connect all those awaiting it. This truth will be presented to those who will rise above personal interests and embrace courage, wisdom, patience, fairness, love, and peace.

I still recall one of my favorite John Suler Zen Stories: **Maybe**.

"There is a Taoist story of an old farmer who had worked his crops for many years. One day his horse ran away. Upon hearing the news, his neighbors came to visit. "Such bad luck," they said sympathetically. "**Maybe**," the farmer replied. The next morning the horse returned, bringing with it three other wild horses. "How wonderful," the neighbors exclaimed. "**Maybe**," replied the old man. The following day, his son tried to ride one of the untamed horses, was thrown and broke his leg. The neighbors again came to offer their sympathy on his misfortune. "**Maybe**," answered the farmer. The day after, military officials came to the village to draft young men into the army. Seeing that the son's leg was broken, they passed him by. The neighbors congratulated the farmer on how well things had turned out. "**Maybe**," said the farmer."

As much as it may be comforting to know that good can come from bad circumstances, it is disturbing to know that bad things can come from good circumstances. But is there good or bad to start within the story, for instance, or is it just what the farmer perceived in his mind?

Whatever the future holds will continue to be unknown and somehow unpredictable because of the uncertainties associated with its various aspects. There may be fewer uncertainties in the material world but more in living things, living things that have "freedom of choice." The knowledge we have about the solar system enables us to predict with high certainty all about the timing and duration of an eclipse, sunrise, day, and night. A system that consists of the materialistic world, living things, and beyond would be predictable to a high degree of certainty only if we possess enough knowledge about it. The only one who can predict the future of such a system is its inventor or the possessor(s) of its entire knowledge.

Challenge Yourself:

- If you could see the future, would you like to keep it as a surprise?

- What if you know that doing the RIGHT thing will result in bad consequences? Would you still decide to do it? (Tip: Risking your life to rescue innocent kids.)

- What if, on the other hand, you know that if you do the wrong thing, your dreams will come true in the future? (Tip: Committing a crime or doing something illegal.)

- Will you be able to change the future if you know what will happen?

One would need to prepare to die every moment by doing the best they can do. The moment that passes will never come back; it is just dead.

When Death Knocks on Your Door

Death is a sensitive topic, isn't it?

Why is it so when it is the only one common destination that we all share and the one thing that we all will experience, at least once? ;)

From the moment of birth, the countdown starts, and everyone awaits the ultimate unifier, a unifier that does not discriminate between the rich and the poor, the weak and the strong, or the good and the bad, etc. The destination itself may be scary, but what may be even scarier to people is what comes afterward.

Those who think their ultimate destination is death may continue to be alive as memories; hopefully good ones.

Although this destination has been reached by billions of human beings with thousands of deaths per day, no one knows much about it nor does anyone know absolutely what comes afterward. The billions who lived and the billions who are still alive have been trying to uncover the mysteries of life they have experienced. Some still strive to unfold what is even more mysterious than life: the deaths they have witnessed. What an irony to have death described only by those who are alive.

Death remains a fascinating and disputable subject among philosophers, theologians, and scientists. Some say we just die (i.e., they live only once), others say we die and come back in one form or another (reincarnation), and others say we never die – death is just a beginning of another life (eternal life that is not physical). None of them can claim to be an expert on death, for there is nothing to know about it.

With the known boundaries of our knowledge and limitations of senses, thinking, and imagination capabilities, no one will ever comprehend the whole story. One may think that it is just intended to be this way to allow everyone to capitalize only on the available knowledge and focus on their strengths while living to do the best in serving themselves, others, and all that is around them. We should not be distracted and waste our time with unknowns, and no one should be judged on what is beyond his or her capacities.

Life is full of examples of "deaths" such as resignations, retirements, divorces, leaving home, or other fundamental change. Although these deaths, even if they were an end to a misery or a start of a joy, are usually harder than anyone may imagine. It is very easy to talk about letting go of things (i.e., transitions), but it is not as easy when the time comes to "depart." It is just so hard to penetrate emotional, mental, habitual, societal and theological walls, or maybe doors/ports. Death is perceived as the final departure to an unknown destination.

In any of these departures, no one should carry sorrows and regrets of the past. They can be the heaviest luggage to carry and they are not needed for the subsequent destination. Instead, one needs to carry a weightless or empty luggage or even better, uplifting "luggage" energized by gratitude, fulfillment, and peace.

Wonder if regret, sorrow, gratitude, fulfillment, and peace have weight!

Some get distracted with life (e.g., work, money, desires, instincts, power) to the extent that death never comes to their minds, as staying alive is taken for granted. Those people need to remember that when death finally knocks on their door, they will see things from many different perspectives. They might witness deaths of family members, friends, and colleagues, or at least they may have seen it via news channels, yet they may never realize that their turn may come at any moment, whatever the cause is. They do not even wonder how many of those whom they met during the last decade might already be dead.

Some have contributed and brought value to humanity, while others have just gone as if they had not even lived. One would need to prepare to die every moment by doing the best they can do. Each moment that passes will never come back; it is just dead. One also needs to understand that obsessive ruminations on death may lead us away from living a quality life. Life and death are the greatest inventions and have to be treated as such.

This reminds me of a story about a conversation between a professor and his old students who visited with him many years after graduation: "Life is Like a Cup of Coffee." "The conversation soon turned into complaints about stress in work and life. Offering his guests coffee, the professor went to the kitchen and returned with a large pot of coffee and an assortment of cups, telling them to help themselves to the coffee.

When each student had a cup of coffee in hand, the professor said: "If you noticed, all the nice looking expensive cups have been taken up, leaving behind the plain and cheap ones. Be assured that the cup itself adds no quality to the coffee. What all of you really wanted was coffee, not the cup, but you consciously went for the best cups. Now consider this: Life is the coffee; the jobs, money and position in society are the cups. They are just tools to hold and contain life, and the type of cup we have does not define, nor change the quality of life we live. Sometimes, by concentrating only on the cup, we fail to enjoy the coffee. Savor the coffee, not the cups! The happiest people do not have the best of everything. They just make the best of everything they have."

Many people, however, perceive that the cup makes a big difference and it even influences how our taste of coffee can be – but life is a combination of both the cup and the coffee. This illusion may disappear if you close your eyes prior to seeing any of the cups. Just taste the coffee from the various cups while your eyes are closed. I am not sure you will notice any difference in the taste of the "same coffee" in them. The students' eyes in the professor's story serve as distracters just as it is the case with many things in life such as clothes, makeup, cars; they might just serve as distracters of what is really significant.

What wisdom would one want from death more than letting one live life to its fullest and living it with no regrets? Death shall be a daily reminder as it may be the upcoming visitor knocking on your door. We must realize that everybody dies, but not everybody lives life to the fullest.

Challenge Yourself:

- If you had to live your life over again, what one thing would you change?
- If you have any regrets in your life, what are the lessons learned?
- Are you prepared to die?

Wish you all a very fulfilling life.

Considering the potential value and power
of integrating differences, integrating a difference
should be considered as an essential, not an optional
goal.

Why Aren't We the Same?

Once upon a time, I felt I had to make a call to a radio show which was discussing a disputable subject. I was a very long-time listener to that show but a first-time caller. I used to listen to the show because I disagreed with most of what the show's host brought and he made me think. Close to the end of the call, he asked me "Why didn't you call earlier?" "I would only call you if I disagree with you or have a different opinion," I replied. "What would the audience gain if all callers agree with you?" I added. "I agree with your thoughts," the host said. I thought that was a good ending of the conversation.

In business, a meeting adds no value to a company if participants have similar opinions; these meetings will only be a waste of resources. The added value comes out of integrating the differences, not the similarities!

Quick demonstrations of the concept: A hand has four fingers and a thumb. They are different in size, length, location, etc. However, they function very well when doing a "task" just because of one reason – they are different. Imagine that all your fingers were "similar" and let's say they would be all thumbs! Would they be able to function as well?

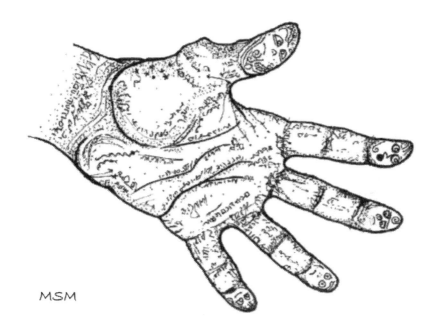

MSM

An adult has a set of 32 teeth that are different. They do function very well when doing a "task" for the same reason and that is only because they are different.

A tribe, a society, a nation, and humanity are composed of people who are different – different colors, sizes, beliefs, tastes, skills, experiences, feelings, cultures, etc. They may all, however, share similar desires, wishes, and needs that can be fulfilled by accomplishing certain "tasks or objectives" such as peace, security, collaboration, harmony, success, and understanding. Diversity needs to be embraced by the human society.

Considering the potential value and power of integrating differences, the human race has no better option but to integrate their differences. That might be why we aren't the same. What is in this simplified concept is a loud call for respect, tolerance, forgiveness, sincerity, and compassion.

"**O mankind!** We created you from a single (pair) of a male and a female, and made you into nations and tribes, that you may know each other. Verily, the most honored of you in the sight of God is (he who is) the most righteous of you." Quran 49: verse 13.

"If the whole body were an eye, where would be the sense of hearing? If the whole body were an ear, where would be the sense of smell?" Corinthians 12:17.

"Iron sharpens iron, and one man sharpens another." Proverbs 27:17.

Challenge Yourself:

- Would you like it if we were all the same?

- Do you see value of diversity?

- Why aren't we the same?

Prior knowledge, mood, experience, personality, and cognitive ability provide a cognitive bias or an anchor when making a decision or judgment. Once this anchor is set, all available information and associated interpretations revolve around it.

If Only We Were One!

We often use the word "know": I know, we know, they know, and you know. "How much do you really know?" my child asked.

One could say that this question is meaningless since there is no sensible way to quantify knowledge. If everyone believes that they possess a great deal of knowledge, then what is it that you really "know" and what percentage of potentially identifiable knowledge do we know?

We may know more about ourselves, less about the physical world around us, and even less about the metaphysical world. Philosophers still wonder where knowledge ultimately comes from (i.e., sources) and the fundamental way(s) of acquiring knowledge beyond the conventional means such as books, media, technologies, cultures, and traditions.

The human race has experienced only a small slice of time, of the universe and of the senses; ironically enough, though, some claim that they have all of the knowledge. Our senses are essential means to acquire the "experimental knowledge," which is only a single source of knowledge.

We have a natural confidence in our senses, and we simply assume that what we see or hear is what exists and what is accurate. Let's examine if this assumption is right.

The human eye can only detect a very small slice of the electromagnetic spectrum, and that is what is called "visible light." Well, many species are different and can see beyond our "visible light," not to mention resolution, distance, etc. The graphic below illustrates the various visible spectrums.

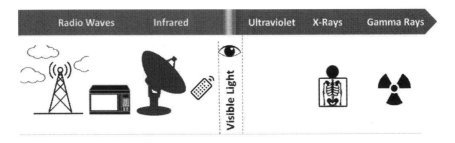

Amazingly enough, we sometimes look at the same thing, but we see it in different colors, as shown in the latest case of the blue-black or white-brown (gold) dress. Yes, we may see "colors" differently, although the colors are within the "visible light." It is not that the colors are different, but it's because of the illusions imposed such as light effects.

The hearing sense is another subject. A human ear is capable of hearing many of the sounds produced in nature, but definitely not all. We can't hear sounds of frequencies below 20 Hz (i.e., infrasound) and can't hear beyond 20,000 Hz (i.e., ultrasound), while many animals can. The graphic below illustrates the various hearing spectrums; and yes again, our hearing sense is limited.

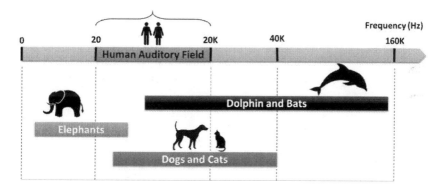

For the sense of touch, I thought of mentioning the famous three containers of water, one filled with warm water, one filled with ambient temperature water, and one filled with ice water. For a minute, one hand is put in the warm container while the other in the cold one, then both are put simultaneously into the middle container, the one filled with ambient temperature water. I am sure you would guess how each hand feels! When describing how each hand feels, it does not matter that the temperature of the middle container is ambient. Be it illusion, confusion, adaption/accustomed, perception, or deception, feelings most of the time unfortunately turn into beliefs.

Would similar consequences occur if our senses of vision, hearing, smelling, or tasting were subject to similar situations? Would our insights, judgments, opinions, and perceptions about things around us also be affected in a similar fashion?

Once again, the influence of the environment and culture on beliefs, and perceptions cannot be overemphasized. Prior knowledge, experience, mood, personality, and cognitive ability provide a cognitive bias or an anchor when making a decision or judgment. Once this **anchor** is set, all available information and associated interpretations revolve around it.

It is very disturbing to "know" that our senses and intellect can be fooled or deceived within their operating envelope (i.e., sensing capabilities), yet some consequences can be catastrophic.

What about other aspects that we cannot even measure: pain, happiness, depression, hope, imagination? What about things beyond the current "known limits" of our knowledge?

One may argue that the maximum accessible knowledge at the current moment is the aggregate of our knowledge if only we were one! Oneness is a competitive advantage for a family, a society, a company, a nation, and humanity. Everyone is not only expected to contribute to the collective oneness but also become part of it.

This cumulative knowledge will eventually alleviate the influence of deceptions on our senses and intellect and potentially make them operate well within their capabilities to bring prosperity and peace to humanity.

Challenge Yourself:

- Are you aware of your biases?
- Do your biases influence your decisions or judgment?
- Would you consciously justify your biases?
- How would one become truly unbiased?

There is not yet a universal definition of life.
All answers can be a controversial subject
among scientists, theologians, and philosophers.

Life is Fair

Who says life is fair!!!???

Hold on to your horses, and let's first define what exactly life is.

What exactly is life?

This seems to be a very basic yet strange question, isn't it?

Well, there isn't yet a universal definition of life. All answers can be controversial. I am sure you all know the word "life," but how would you define life? It can be defined as the period between birth and death, or the state of being alive, but there are many other meanings.

Biologists, for instance, determine what living things share in common. Living things consume energy, grow, reproduce, evolve, and produce waste. But mules are living animals, yet they don't demonstrate all the attributes; they do not reproduce! Most proposed definitions of life tend to have loopholes, just like in the story of the blind men touching a different part of an elephant to learn what the whole elephant is like.

It is so mind-boggling to realize that cells, the basic unit of all living things, are made up of non-living matter (i.e., dead matter), and all life forms share fundamental molecular mechanisms that reflect one common origin. Would this mean that every living thing is made of similar "dead matter"? An observer may ask if everything that is living in this universe is made of similar dead matter, would this living thing be considered dead or alive? And how could anything die if it was not initially alive?

We are only aware of one form of life, and it does not make sense to generalize it on this basis and claim to have full comprehension of what life is. Life will only be defined if it can be recreated from nothing. Then, one may possess the complete knowledge to be able to define it, describe its beginning, and possibly explains its end (i.e., death), if it even has an end. Although death is perceived as the permanent termination of life processes, many religions maintain faith in either a kind of afterlife or reincarnation for the soul, or a resurrection of the body.

One of the challenges in defining death is in distinguishing it from life. Death is referred to as either the moment life ends, or when the state that follows life begins. However, determining when death has occurred requires drawing precise conceptual boundaries between life and death. This is problematic again as we have indicated, since there isn't a consensus on how to define life, how it began, or how it will end. This has been a concern of the world's religious traditions, of philosophical inquiry, and scientific research.

The life force that drives bodies remains a mystery. This force or energy, which has never been seen, separates from the body at the moment of death, leaving a body with no life. The dead body retains all the physical matter of living body (e.g., cells, DNA, organs, brain), but life symptoms (movement, personality, purpose, etc.) depart the vessel (i.e., body) when death arrives. It is clear that life energy is not physical in nature. If the law of conservation of energy still holds, then this energy is transformed into another form. Once all sorts of energies reach equilibrium, it will be the time where everything, living or dead, moves to its right place (i.e., that is fair).

The universe is in "equilibrium" from its beginning until its end, and so is life. On this earth, there is enough air for everyone to breathe, enough food to eat, enough water to drink, enough resources to use, and enough places to live in. There is enough for any living thing to live comfortably and in equilibrium.

One may shout loudly: "Life is not fair; don't you see poverty in the world, injustice, wars, starvation, destruction, difficulties, sorrows, accidents, failures, catastrophes, discrimination!?" In a lifetime, we witness "unfair" things that we can't understand or justify; no one denies them. They are all made by man, who immorally causes disturbances to the equilibriums and life has nothing to do with it. The man-made disturbance, although it hurts, is merely a **temporary** one.

The comprehension of life is bounded by our limitations and the limited knowledge that we have. Until the moment we define it and realize the essence of it and describe its boundaries; I can comfortably say that "life is fair" unless proven otherwise.

Challenge Yourself:

- What is life?
- What is fairness?
- Assuming you believe that "life is NOT fair, what would be your contribution to making it fair?

I really don't possess the answers, and all I have are questions for you to think about. Thinking is not yet forbidden, my dear readers, and it is among the rare things that makes one alive. Wish you all a very fulfilling "life."

We, together, ought to build an "ark of salvation,"
a ship that does not sink.
The alternative is a sinking ship.

Sinking Ships

From the earliest civilizations to the modern times, ships have served scientific, technological, cultural, naval, commercial, environmental, recreational, and humanitarian purposes. Countless ships have been built but only a few of them have made it into history with a lasting impact. I am certain that all respected readers have heard about at least a few. Among the famous ships are the Titanic that sank in the North Atlantic Ocean in 1912 after hitting a massive iceberg, the German battleship (the Bismarck), the USS Arizona and Maine, and "Noah's Ark." The stories of these ships were the material of movies, books, stories, and agendas – they have an everlasting impact that extends beyond their times and beyond those who were on board. The will always be remembered and framed or articulated in various ways in order to serve a purpose.

Say a ship is any vehicle or conveyance. Say it is a vessel, carrier, or a means by which we travel through space or time. These "vessels" can be physical (your body, car, house, company, country, earth, etc.), social/cultural/moral (family, people), financial (business, funds), mental (thoughts), spiritual (beliefs), and emotional (feelings). The irony is that many of the remembered ships are those that sank or were abandoned. Of course, the actual intent of any ship is not to stay at a harbor or sink during a journey, but to safely navigate and arrive at its destination, as it was the case with "Noah's Ark." Who does not want to be on board a ship similar to "Noah's Ark"?

The phrase "a sinking ship" is used with reference to deteriorating conditions/decay (e.g., biological, physiological, social, financial, environmental, political, personal, etc.) aspects. When facing a great crisis or even at the first sign of trouble or before it gets too bad, most will turn and run just like rats deserting/abandoning a sinking ship. One may observe this happening in stock markets, failing companies, broken families or relationships – members just disengage from the "club." Some observers would say that "rats" have great ability to predict the future and possess foreknowledge of the ship's doom, and they do not want to be on board when it is going down. They'd rather take their chances in the open water. ;)

It takes loyalty, courage, guts, and stubbornness, or maybe just enough stupidity to stay on board a sinking ship. Those who are afraid of water cannot prevent a ship from sinking and will most probably "sink" with it.

Any "vessel" is subjected to both internal and external forces. Qualified captains and prepared crews have full control of the internal forces, and they have to regulate and adjust their strategies and activities to capitalize on the external forces as much as possible. They are not only expected but also responsible for keeping the ship in equilibrium and stable in all conditions. Instability issues may lead to excessive pitching and capsizing. One reasonably understands that external forces may not be within anybody's circle of influence, but will always trust that internal forces are.

There are numerous stories about ships, mostly reported by missionaries, anthropologists, and ethnologists. Many of them have a common ESSENCE. One of the more famous stories talks about passengers who boarded a ship sailing in a river. Some of the passengers stayed on the deck, while others stayed down below, within the hull. Whenever the latter group needed water, they had to go up through the deck to get water. To avoid going through the deck, they decided to dig a hole through the hull (i.e., their part of the ship) to get water. If they were left to dig the hole, the ship would most probably sink. However, if they were prevented from digging the hole, the ship and all passengers would be safe. Many people would tend to dig that hole in the ship, even when they know that it would destroy them because their ego/pride will not let them do otherwise.

Among the most dangerous crews' deficiencies are the following: inexperience, arrogance, lack of preparation, lack of focus, and lack of rules – and may also include not knowing the destination or the most direct routes. It's a pity that such unqualified crews do not possess the intuition that rats have, and they do not realize that there are more ways to die than survive when life puts one in such circumstances.

This ship can be a symbol of great civilization. When the factors that led to the decline of social, cultural, financial and moral values of an ancient civilization are assessed and understood, one can comprehend their disastrous consequences. Realizing that similar patterns can be found in many civilizations, one would realize that what happened to them can happen to us unless we learn from history and act accordingly to prevent a repeat. People must know who is sailing the ship of their lives!

Ships exist in different shapes, sizes, specifications, and capabilities.   Passengers, including crews on these different ships, need to put their hands together to safely sail. When the ship is hurt, everyone on board will also be hurt. This sums up the principles of solidarity, tolerance, shared responsibility, integration, and collaboration need to keep the ship safe, in equilibrium and stable. Isn't prevention always better than the cure?

The story of Noah and his faith had him build the ark before the flood came. All the people thought he was crazy. It took him decades to build the ship, and at a time when a ship would not be considered to ever be needed. He was on the right ship, and everyone else was on the wrong ship. It must have been very hard for him to stay the course when all the wind was against him, but those are the times that leaders stand up and keep going against the mainstream.

Many cultures have a tradition of global flood stories. The flood is a symbol of results of deteriorating conditions, and the ship is a symbol of a means of salvation. Whatever the ship looks like, one wants to board a reliable, safe, and non-sinking ship with dynamic positioning to be able to navigate and venture into the deepest parts of seas and oceans without fear or doubts that they will be safe.

We, **together**, ought to build the "ark of salvation," the ship that does not sink. The alternative is a sinking ship.

Challenge Yourself:

- Are you sailing the ship of your life?

- What if you have discovered you are on board the wrong ship?

- What would you do and how would you feel if you and your family were on board a sinking ship?

Children, animals, insects, and fish
see no borders through their innocent eyes.

Borderless!

Borders can be real or virtual lines that confine the inside or outside boundaries of an "area" or a subject of interest. These lines can be geographical, technological, natural, special, temporal, historical, political, and even psychological. They separate or describe the extent of shapes, surfaces, countries, states, provinces, cities, homes, rooms, times, cultures, languages, etc.

They function very well as leading indicators of a potential sudden change, an edge or a "wall." All geometric shapes (cubes, pyramids, etc.) have edges except for one shape which I find very amazing: the sphere. Maybe the earth was meant to be "spherical."

Every person or a nation tries to have its "possessions" protected, controlled, organized, and/or isolated. They all have the right to do so; however, one may wonder why some national borders are very loose while others have strict regulations. All of these borders are man-made, and man is the only one who decides how they are defined and applied, and when they can change. These changes can either make nations stronger or weaker, richer or poorer, protected or vulnerable, peaceful or violent. It is such a strange and mind-boggling reality to see how these lines that are man-made can be so influential in creating virtual borders in MINDS and EMOTIONS with almost similar consequences.

This article does not advocate changing existing borders, eliminating them, or changing existing policies; however, it challenges respected readers to deeply think about them, their history, and their positive or adverse impacts while honoring and preserving the value of diversity, differences, security, and ownership.

On this pretty earth, no creature decides where and when it is born, no one chooses its own parents, culture, or country, and no one designates their genes. They should not be a source of pride nor should they be a cause of shame. Children, animals, insects, and fish see no borders through their innocent eyes. Birds freely fly across borders (incredible seasonal moves). Salmon travel across waters salty and sweet to build their nest, lay their eggs, and die (fascinating life and epic journey).

Light, air, dust, rain, thunder, earthquakes, volcanoes, hurricanes see no borders. Good or bad feelings, knowledge, and science cross all known physical borders. Nowadays, cyberspace is virtually making the world borderless!

It is making the dynamic overlap between some of these borders (e.g., political, cultural, and psychological) bigger and a bit harder to draw. The cyber world has demonstrated how it is possible to live with no borders in both good and evil ways. One might dream or imagine that this borderless cyberspace world might one day converge into one "culture," one "ideology," and one "language." This has already manifested itself in video games. In this hypothetical situation, some will elect to adopt the "microbiologist's" approach described in the below brain teaser. :)

Once upon a time, a farmer challenged an engineer, a physicist, and a microbiologist to fence off the largest amount of area using the least amount of fence.

The engineer made his fence in a circle and said it was the most efficient. The physicist made a long line and said that the length was infinite. Then he said that fencing half of the earth was the best. The microbiologist laughed at the others and with his design, beat them. He made a small fence around himself and declared himself to be on the outside of the largest possible area.

Back to physical borders…

People may dispute whether (1) borders would be obstacles towards better communication, health, collaboration, understanding, and exchange, and hence work towards one, the common good, resulting in a "better world" for EVERYONE; or (2) borders are necessities and created for a reason to secure resources, traditions, ideologies, or limit illegal trafficking, etc. They still see that these borders should not deprive people from forming a peaceful and tolerant world where people love others within their own borders and those beyond -- assuming people within similar borders are free of prejudice, united, and love each other!

Imagine you are the only person on earth; how would you want the world to be, a borderless world or not? Any border would be meaningless then. That was exactly how the world originally began and this is exactly how it will end.

Always remember that you are an important part of this world. You can make a difference, a good difference -- whether the world is kept with borders or it becomes **_BORDERLESS_**.

Challenge Yourself:

- Is it hypothetically possible to have the real world with no borders, and what would be the impact?
- What would it take and what would be required to have a world with no borders?
- Would you be scared if people have unrestricted mobility?
- Would you SINCERELY accept the world to be borderless and why?

This universal consensus about the name of colors
has not been influenced by histories, ideologies,
theologies, ethnicities, conflicts, borders, or skin colors.

Colorful

When we look at skies, water, mountains, trees, and rainbows; when we see people, animals, birds, fish and insects – we see pieces of spectacular colorful paintings.

Have you ever thought about how we see the colors of these paintings?

Have you ever wondered if we all see colors the same way?

Let's start this article by a simple test. :)

Would you name the colors of the following squares?

The answers will definitely be similar (I guess), and if anyone is in doubt, any coloring program/tool (e.g., colorimeter or spectrophotometer) with capabilities to identify colors will remove that doubt. Eventually, everyone will have similar answers even if what they see is different due to internal or external reasons (e.g., color deficiency or light effects). What is so amazing about these colors is that all of them are reflections of one colorless and invisible thing that we call light. This colorless light mystically

152

decomposes into colors of the spectrum as seen in a rainbow. It is truly amazing!

The ability to see colors is a very complex process, yet most of us take it for granted and don't even think about it. This sophisticated process to translate light into colors is a product of an intelligent design and seamlessly interwoven functions between the human eye and the brain. The eye alone does not convey the whole story. One may argue that it is not important to know the details of the structure of an eye nor is it important to study how we see as long we all share a common name of every color.

I find it fascinating to study the structure of the eye and not to believe that it is a product of an intelligent design. Let's briefly zoom into the eye and study how we see colors. We may have a greater sense of appreciation to one of the many gifts we were born with: the eyes.

The process of seeing color is incredible. Our eyes are not sensitive to light with wavelengths shorter than 400 nanometers (violet light) or longer than around 700 nanometers (red light). When light within the visible light spectrum bounces off objects into the cornea, then goes through the pupil, it goes through the lens that angles and focuses the light on the outer layer of the retina where millions of light-sensitive cells (the photoreceptors) called rods and cones are located.

Cones and rods are two types of cells sensitive to light. Rods are responsible for our perception of light and dark, and they can't distinguish colors, while cones allow us to see colors and exist in three kinds: red, green and blue (RGB). Both rods and cones convert light into electro-chemical signals that are sent via the optic nerve to the brain for processing and interpretation.

Although most people have three types of cones, some people (mostly male) have only two cones. It is those who we call colorblind, who have trouble distinguishing red from green. Animals' eyes also have similar anatomy to that of a human's eyes. While some animals have two cones, others such as birds have four kinds of cones and some, such as shrimp, have up to 12 different kinds of cones. Scientists are not certain how these animals perceive colors or if all these cones are used. What has recently been discovered is that a few people possess four kinds of cones, and that makes them potentially capable of seeing more colors than what "normal" people see. As much as it is hard for colorblind people to experience and imagine how "normal" people see green and red, it is hard for "normal" people to experience what a person with four cones can see. Scientists may discuss this subject theoretically and generate a scientific/theoretical image of what the world looks like through the different eyes, but they will always remain uncertain about it unless they experience it.

You know that none of these eyes can see colors in the dark nor can they see when they are exposed to a light flash of extremely high intensity. When it is absolutely dark, it would be impossible to see anything. Even when light exists, one would need to be aware that a normal eye, the brain, and the mind might be tricked and influenced by the external and internal environments (e.g., surrounding colors, type of light, shadows, teachings, ideologies, experience, and culture). The mind in this context is defined as the interpreter of images and colors, where images or colors are formed in the minds, than by what is seen through the eyes and processed through the brain. The whole world calls the color red because they were all taught that it is red. Imagine that a whole society calls white black. They see it white but call it black. Everyone calls it black. They would call it black because they were taught that this color was black, and this is when white may become black in their view.

We are fortunate enough to have a universal consensus about the name of colors. Yes, white is always white and black is always black. This is among the rare consensuses humans have reached, and this consensus has not been influenced by histories, ideologies, theologies, ethnicities, conflicts, borders, or skin colors.

There is another "set of colors" that are only seen by the internal eye. History has not shown that a similar consensus to that of the above could be reached nor does a specialized colorimeter or spectrophotometer exist to resolve disputes about "colors." The perceptions of these colors are very much influenced by teachings, culture, upraising, conflicts, and feelings.

It is so sad to realize that when these internal eyes become "blind" and stop seeing colors the way they are trained to be, all they can see are fairness, love, peace, care and compassion. They may become blind when it becomes absolutely dark or when they are exposed to "a light flash of extremely high intensity" (i.e. catastrophes; big catastrophes). It is only during these times one would observe the vanishing impact of all the influencing teachings and almost everyone follows their instinctive humanitarian behaviors. Natural catastrophes often unite families, neighbors, and even nations. Many people would blindly help each other, save each other, and provide food, clothes, and shelters to each other. This is evident during hurricanes, tsunamis, earthquakes, etc.

Sadly enough, when a catastrophe is over, the internal eye gradually sees the way it used to see. One may wish that catastrophes continue for a nation to be united and wish that they get used to it until it becomes a habit. But this is not what is meant by life. Life is meant to be colorful, and we were meant to see these colors the same way through both our internal and external eyes. We were all meant to see black as black, white as white, red as red, blue as blue, "right as right," "wrong as wrong," "bad as bad," "good as good," "peace as peace," and "war as war." One of the ways to see colors the way they are is to strive to be erudite, wise, caring, empathetic, and conscientiously free from prejudice, greed, and hate until you see colors through your own eyes rather than seeing colors through someone else's eye, an eye that might be blind.

Challenge Yourself:

- Is it true that "color" doesn't matter?
- Would you be able to consciously choose to see no colors through your internal eye?
- "*The People United will Never be Defeated.*" Do you foresee that people will ever be united? Why not or how?

A major emotional event, a shock, more of a burning
platform or more of "Change or Die" situation
may be required to significantly shift an individual's,
societies' or company's belief system.

When Organizations Become Pregnant

Numerous studies and research describe how individuals, societies, cultures, and /or corporations inherit attributes and have them embedded in their beliefs and intellectual models, like having them implanted in their genes.

Some of these attributes have been developing since the onset of time; one would be too ambitious or egotistical to think that these attributes could drastically change.

There are many publications about organizational culture, change management and cultural beliefs... with many experts introducing various approaches to facilitate smoother and more-effective cultural changes. Cultural change remains as one of the most difficult challenges. We may be able to develop programs that allow people to know what we need to change, what we desire to accomplish and the potential impact of these changes on current culture or business environment. Would that be enough? Of course not.

What is required is to change the way we behave and the way we communicate, which is a clear translation of how we THINK. So, it boils down into one thing: the "way we think." How would that be possible?

A major emotional event, a shock, more of a burning platform or more of "Change or Die" situation may be required to significantly shift an individual's, societies' or company's belief system. These events are very rare, and they are not the sort of events deliberately created in order to make people change.

Let's have some real examples here for the sake of clarification. What if you were told you need to make a change or you would die? You would certainly do it. Who wouldn't?

Ironically, most people would not. Even when not changing means death, we are immune even to change-or-die messages. A rather vivid example of this has to do with people who undergo bypass surgery. The surgery is an invasive, painful procedure. In many cases of bypass surgery or angioplasty, the procedures end up failing to protect patients against future heart attacks. Why? Not because the procedures were inherently flawed. The high failure rate occurs because high percentage of post-intervention patients do not sustain behavioral lifestyle changes necessary to help these invasive procedures do their job, even in the face of being told they will likely either need further surgery or die if they do not. What that means is that temporary changes introduced by enhancements in processes may seem to make progress but will eventually be drawn back into the existing culture. It means that the "burning platform" has limited effectiveness, and we should no longer rely on occasional ad hoc programs to accomplish the desired everlasting change. If a change is seriously needed in an organization, for instance, the approach has to be significantly different, and it has to be executed across an entire corporation and continuously at all levels.

Change is not a "mission impossible," but it is a very challenging mission. I am sure that most of the readers of this article want to challenge paradigms and to make a difference.

So let me bring another example that I think may provide further wisdom. The medical industry has great examples that are analogous to our subject. Let's consider a "change" as an implant, a foreign/external body.

Once this implant is applied, it disturbs an existing equilibrium state of a body (body = a society, a religion, a culture, or a corporation). Once this equilibrium is affected, even if the implant/change is introduced for worthy reasons, a call is initiated to the immune system to fight against it. That is just a natural process during which the body recognizes an invasion by an external foreign object.

In the human body, the various organs involved work together to constantly maintain a stable internal environment/equilibrium. Under ideal conditions, the implant (induced change) should not cause any undesired reaction. However, implants can adversely impact equilibrium, leading to complications and awakening of the human body immune system. Among the implications are infection, inflammation, and pain. Other complications that can occur include risk of rejection from implant-induced coagulation and allergic foreign body response. Depending on the type of implant, the complications may vary based on the physical and chemical nature of the implants and could sometimes lead to catastrophic results.

In general, the human body reacts to foreign objects (changes) in ways to get rid of them. Even if the implants were made from an INERT material, the immune system would be activated to at least respond to a normal wound-healing process and might require extended courses of antibiotics. Luckily, the medical industry has significantly improved in this arena and continues to improve.

An observer may ask: "I realize that it is very complicated to implant a foreign object in human body. Then, how would a pregnant female conceive and nourish within herself with a fetus that is anti-genetically different, and how would the immune system react in a way that commonly promotes successful pregnancy and not an immune rejection of a foreign body? The pregnancy biological process has been successful since the onset of time and has proven its robustness. The process still works."

Paradoxically, the immune system does not really halt but recognizes pregnancy and evidently ADAPTS and determines the success or failure of it. This particular subject has been of great interest to scientists, who would like to uncover more about consequences of the adaptation of the immune system and its complex responses during pregnancy. The magnificence of the whole process is that it is an entirely INTERNAL, dynamic, connected, adaptable and effective process, one that goes beyond the physical boundaries. It is not governed by the laws of physics only, but considers various dimensions: emotional, mental, physiological, spiritual, social, and ethical. What really impedes this process is CARE. Leaders of effective organizational changes do care and consider all the internal dimensions when planning for a change. Some business managers, however, unconsciously impose organizational changes which consider fewer dimensions or are only governed by "physics laws" that are external. The changes done by the former are born to last, while the latter induced by external forces never last and will be gone once the external forces disappear. Although the logic may be applicable to all business, I must associate the logic with some aspects of the technological world and the changes associated with its ever-changing technologies and their applications.

Technologies have surely brought more demand for changes, and I don't see signs that this pace of change will slow down. The changes these technologies bring demand for modifications in the way we manage projects, communities, HR, processes, communication, operations, etc. Whatever the situation is, the essential competencies that governments, solidities, and organizations need include not only to know what needs to be changed but to have the capacity to effectively execute the required changes with a dynamic vision and continuous care that are infused into their genes. I am sure experts in change management can educate various stakeholders on the most effective approaches to fulfill their goals. They must make sure that the change is internal in order to facilitate continuous care; that is, when you have any immune system working for them, not against them.

Gandhi once said, "Be the change you want to see in the world." When everyone in a community, nation, or an organization becomes the "change," that will be the time **when organizations become pregnant**.

Challenge Yourself:

- How easy is it to change perceptions?
- What would expedite changes in social values?
- What drives people resistance to change?

Beware that many people to a certain extent are "asleep."
The only time they will see reality the way it is,
is when they wake up to discover that
they have been living in a world of zombies.

Wake Up... You May Be Living in a World of Zombies

Have you ever wondered what might be there in the deepest points of the oceans, the highest peaks of mountains, or what might be there in the skies? Have you ever wondered how scientists could precisely describe a star or a planet that is millions of light-years away and know when it was born, what it is made of and what its future might be?

With all the history man has on earth and all the advancements man has witnessed, man will never be able to fully explore the world, let alone the universe. The irony is that scientists have not been successful in exploring and uncovering the mysteries of man's fascinating internal worlds. These mysteries become even

169

harder to uncover when we enter the relatively unknown world of sleep, a world that takes a third of our lifetime. Philosophers, scientists, and researchers do not know what world we go to when we are asleep, they don't know what sleep is, and they don't even know why we sleep.

We can stand here forever wondering what sleep is, or we can take an adventure trying to discover its wonders… as if we ever could. This reoccurring adventure is experienced by all of the living things, and it begins when we mysteriously become completely detached from the world we live in and lose all the conscious relationships with the materialistic world. The theories about this world experience are numerous. Some suggest that it is an uninterrupted, unconscious resting time for our body and mind. Others suggest that it is a restorative process for the body, and some research suggests that it relieves, reenergizes, and heals the brain. Whatever the reality is, many organisms miraculously never sleep – truly mind-boggling!!

Sleep, like death, is an inexorable fair master, possibly the master of all masters, in that does not distinguish between the poor and rich, young and old, male and female, or a king and a slave. All of them go through the same journey almost every day not knowing how this journey will end. Sleep begins when muscles start to relax (i.e., first stage), and go through various stages until reaching the REM (Rapid Eye Movement) stage when the brain becomes very active. This is the time when dreams occur, and it is the time when one enters an even more mysterious world, the world of dreams. Every stage of sleep is unique in every cycle of sleep. These cycles tend to repeat more than once every night.

The world of dreams has also been a subject of contemplation and research by scientists, philosophers, psychologists, and theologians. Throughout recorded history, they have come up with various explanations for dreaming, as well as the meanings of dreams. It remains among the mysteries that are yet to be solved. Some scientists suggest that dreams are just reflections of actual activities or feelings. Others suggest that they are simply the results of random brain activities.

When you dream, everything appears real and lucid just like it is when you are awake, doesn't it? You talk, you walk, you touch, you feel, and even sweat. You fly like a bird with no wings, swim as a fish with no gills, walk on water, speak languages you don't really know, and have things you don't really possess. You may dream as if you were in your mother's womb, a baby, a teenager, an old person, or even dead. You may dream that one day there will be peace. You may have a dream within a dream. Once awake, one would realize that it was just a dream and may wonder if the same thing happens in "real life" and how real this life is. Would it be possible that one day we become awake and realize that our "real life" is just a dream? Everything looks equally vivid and real as perceived through the minds, minds that are anchored to and influenced by a set of deeply ingrained beliefs.

Dreams are not only limited to those images that come during sleep at night; they can be the illusions/daydreams we have while we are awake – that is if we are really awake. Many people become mindless and sleepwalk through their lives just like zombies. Zombies, in the simplest form, are unintelligent, un-dead corpses. In some of the early movies, the zombies' appearance was similar to that of the living, yet they were silent, slow, and mindlessly submitting to and controlled by a wicked master, a master who could be an influencer, a parent, a teacher, a politician, or those in power.

ZSM

In the movies, zombies could not be eliminated unless their brain was destroyed, they wanted to devour real human flesh, and sadly enough, any normal human became a zombie once bitten by a zombie. Although single zombies are weak and lack brain power, they become dangerous in large numbers and in confined spaces. These confined spaces can be homes, societies, organizations, nations or even the whole world. Aren't they all led and managed by people? Hopefully not zombies. What can be so devastating in real life is that some healthy people live under the illusion that they are sick, live rich lives under the illusion that they are poor, or kings live under the illusion that they are slaves. The worst among all are those who live under the illusion they are angels, rescuers, and peacemakers while they are servants of the devil, if not real devils.

There will always be multiple versions of how the world looks. These versions are influenced by where we are, who we are, and the decisions we make, as well as by many other factors; no wonder every one of us has unique perceptions about realities. We do change all the time and so do our perceptions of "realities."

We are not who we were ten years ago. We have been replaced by multiple versions of ourselves including our bodies, minds, insights, emotional states, preferences, perspectives, principles, and mindsets. Some changes are abrupt; and some are invisible, slow, and unnoticeable, yet they seamlessly happen even during the time we are asleep. The person we are in this morning is different from the one who went to bed last night. In order to truly be awake, one needs to be insightful, thoughtful, empathetic, resourceful, respectful, grateful, and fair, and needs to be always reminded that life is not a dream, a thought, a perception, or a feeling.

Your life, just like anyone else's, will not be set until you fully comprehend that your version of reality is highly influenced by the reflections of your perceptions of things beyond the distracting materialistic world. Be aware that many people to a certain extent are "asleep." The only time they will see reality the way it is, is when they wake up to discover that they have been living in a world of zombies.

"The body experiences six different states: health, sickness, death, life, sleep, and wakefulness, and so does the spirit. Its life is its knowledge, its death is ignorance, its sickness is doubt, its health is certainty, its sleep is negligence and its wakefulness is consciousness." – Imam Ali.

Challenge Yourself:

- Have you ever witnessed a zombie?
- Are you influenced by day dreaming?
- What would you do if you realize that you are living in a world of zombies?

There is not a big difference between
career and personal experiences,
as both resemble exploratory journeys
to discover the sources of treasures.

Mining for Hidden Treasures

Mining for stone and metal has existed since the beginning of civilization. Most of earth's natural treasures form in the earth's crust hundreds and thousands of meters beneath the earth's surface. The "mining" industries and scientists have evolved and developed advanced mining methods and technologies to uncover the myriads of hidden treasures. Any mining endeavor is always expensive and the associated efforts are immense. People mine for oil and gas, coal, metal and non-metallic minerals (e.g., precious stones). In essence, it requires mining to get treasures. With the advancements of the various industries, an abundance of new forms of virtual precious stones have come into existence and this time, these "precious stones" exist in the "minds" of machines (i.e., data, Bitcoin).

In the petroleum business, for instance, exploration, drilling, and completion have to be done before getting the first drop of oil (i.e., treasure). These are all efforts done in order to get that drop and sometimes explorers end up getting nothing. It is rare to find such treasures without "drilling." A similar process is used to extract knowledge from large volumes of raw data by a combination of tools from AI, statistics, and database management. The most

177

evident use of data mining is in businesses such as retail, scientific research, and security.

There is not a big difference between career and personal experiences, as both resemble exploratory journeys to discover the sources of treasures.

One would need to mine in his/her own "mind" for treasures too, and that takes time and effort. I feel that I have to not only whisper in your ears, but also say it loud enough that everyone hears my message: There are more of these treasures in you, around you, and almost everywhere than you ever thought of.

I would like to use this article to share with you some of the treasures I have found during my career and personal life.

I have learned that those who challenged me are those who made me stronger.

I have learned that we always have a choice when facing a challenge: We can make excuses why it cannot be done or we can spend the same amount of energy figuring out how it can be done.

I have learned that one would think and learn more if engaged in a disagreement but would not learn anything when it is otherwise. Working in multidisciplinary teams is wonderful. It gives us easy access to see things differently through fresh eyes.

I have learned to look to my comrades, mentors, and those who have trained me, drawing strength from them. I will always cherish their prestige, honor, and respect.

I have learned that every moment of life is very precious as it provides a chance to practice self-mastery and control by expanding visions, awakening the senses of our minds and our hearts, and assuming full responsibility for living, growing, and making contributions. It does not come by accident. Change and patience are two distinct challenges but neither are impossible.

I have learned that knowledge is power. It is very easy to get confused, especially when one knows too little. I am sure that those who know nothing are usually not confused. One should recognize choices in life but must take responsibility for his/her decisions.

I have learned ways to challenge and overcome conventional assumptions that block growth, and I have learned a generation of solutions that led to development and success.

I have learned that one's accomplishments are neither given nor inherited; they are earnings that no one will deny and no one will defy. I can declare that (P.E.A.C.E.): Passion, Effort, Awareness, Commitment, and Enthusiasm are five ingredients that can lead to success. What is even more important is the sense of ownership.

I have learned that it is easy to become so preoccupied with work and other commitments that you lose sight of the importance of many issues like parents, family, community, and friends.

I have learned the secret. The secret is in you as it translates in your daily life as the virtual images you have in your mind. Think positively, and focus intently, then like a magnet, you will be attracting things you are passionate about.

I have been mining for hidden treasures during my life, and I believe I have what I can call a treasure. I know that there will always be more to discover and to mine for. Remember, "One does not discover new lands without consenting to lose sight of the shore for a very long time," Andre Gide said.

I have learned that you get as much as you give. I would like to thank you, the readers of this article, for taking the time to read it. If it were not for you, the treasure I had mined for would not have any value.

Challenge Yourself:

- I am sure every one of you possesses a treasure. Would you be so kind to share one of your "precious stones" with others?
- "If you have an apple and I have an apple and we exchange these apples then you and I will still each have one apple. But if you have an idea and I have an idea and we exchange these ideas, then each of us will have two ideas." George Bernard Shaw.

Those who wear masks slowly become immersed in fake virtual lives till they lose sight of who they really are and the masks they wear. They become unconsciously unaware of the adverse impacts on themselves and others.

Wear No Mask!

The origin of masks or the idea of covering or disguising the human face has been traced to prehistoric man. Depictions of masks have been found in caves, rock paintings, artifacts, literature, and traditions of almost all of the known cultures around the world. Masks were created in different shapes, sizes, and colors and they have been used for a variety of objectives.

They can be religious, protective, ritualistic, spiritual, political, tribal, ceremonial, medical, theatrical, social, criminal, or just facial. Some of the earlier uses of masks portrayed the various moods embossed on human faces as reflections of the experiences of the emotions and the states of the mind: love, hope, anger, hate, fury, fear, disgust, etc.

If we are not confined by the stereotypes of being hypocritical appearances, old masks could reflect purity, innocence, and simplicity of primitive man. Considering the ancient Latin word for mask, "persona," that literally translates to "false face," an aspect of the personality shown to or perceived by others; one may argue that everyone who wears a mask is a hypocrite to some degree!

In this article, I am not writing about the details about old masks from different regions of the world and how they have been fascinating, expressive, or primitive. Neither will I be writing about medical, facial, beauty, façade, or protective masks. The article will discuss different types of masks but not the physical ones.

The damage that **PHYSICAL** masks cause even if they were misrepresented or misused is very limited. The potential damage comes from **VIRTUAL** masks that almost everyone wears in the course of a day that act as a disguise to get through a variety of situations in their personal or career life. Although these masks may be used to protect privacy, gain social acceptance, hide pain, hide fear, etc., they can also be misused as a tool for deception, trickery, rebellion, oppression, evil, and corruption.

The new media industry, including "cyber-cultures," is an excellent microcosm for the manifestation of the masks people wear. Common examples of cyber-cultures include websites such as online newspaper feeds, blogs, social media, and others. The masks used in these cyber-cultures, cyber societies, and/or cyber communities may be used to disguise an individual's real identity so as to temporarily become someone different to fulfill hidden desires. Some wear multiple masks to project *IDEAL* virtual selves into different platforms such as Facebook, LinkedIn, SnapChat, Twitter, Instagram, and others.

They wear them to become somewhat *anonymous*, to feel a fake sense of freedom, security, privacy, and maybe gutsy enough to uncover some of the hidden aspects of their personality that can't be expressed in "conservative" situations.

Some may say that "a mask makes it easier for you to be your real self." Others may argue why some people become different when they no longer wear masks. An observer will always be puzzled about who the "real selves" of those who wear masks are. Those who wear masks slowly become immersed in fake virtual lives till they lose sight of who they really are and the masks they wear. They become unconsciously unaware of the adverse impacts on themselves and others. People respect and connect with real people who share their genuine selves and have the integrity to be who they are in all circumstances.

Some justify their disguise to ensure privacy, security, and anonymity so that their activities can't be tracked. Well, there isn't anything that can keep one absolutely anonymous, not only in the open web but even in the dark, deep, or invisible web.

It is not very practical nor is it realistic to eliminate these masks completely, since masks may sometimes be used for decent objectives. But one must know that masks, most of the time, cause harm.

"We all wear masks and the time comes when we cannot remove them without removing some of our own skin." – André Berthiaume.

The impact of the "masks" can become more catastrophic when the wearers of masks are among the influencers including politicians, religious leaders, teachers, authors, speakers, celebrities, icons, movie or sports stars, etc., individuals who have mass followers or may be "slaves." If you closely examine what is happening around the world and if we are able see through masks, the true faces will bring a large majority of these influencers to shame.

These "influencers" in your life wield an enormous influence on your values, beliefs, thoughts, views, and opinions so frequently that you unconsciously become their own slave, singing their song and echoing their voices. Imagine that you reach the end of your life not realizing how your personal preferences are not originally yours but are based on disguised influencers. That is very scary, isn't it?

It is very hard for any of us to acknowledge that there are people who influence and possibly control how we make our most important choices in life. The bottom line is that no one will fight your inner battle(s) for you; you are the only trustworthy soldier to continuously fight your own battles. I am sure that the struggle is worth it, knowing that a single life that is worth living is a genuine life, a finite journey, during which one would be blessed to figure out what "a genuine life" means.

Respected reader, you are somehow, somewhere, and sometimes an influencer, an influencer with a great power beyond what you may imagine. Remember that with more power, the more responsible you must become.

Always keep looking at the mirror and make sure you **wear no mask**!

"Pretending to be someone you are not is a waste of the person you are." – Kurt Cobain.

Challenge Yourself:

- What would make you wear a mask? Why?
- Would you be able to live without wearing a mask?
- If wearing masks does not harm anyone, would that be OK?

It all boils down to fear that resides within invisible walls, the walls constructed in our minds.
Sometimes, we have to do what we are scared of doing.

Resistance

What a word! A word with multiple meanings!

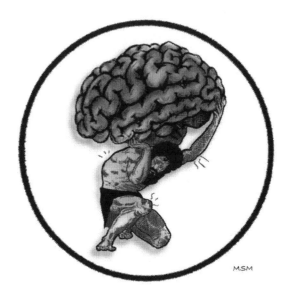

A polysemic word is any word that possesses multiple definitions, different applications, and different concepts. One may ask: If a word has multiple meanings, is it a single word with multiple meanings or is it different words? Well, dictionaries show such words as one word and thus one may be able to accurately identify the number of words in a language. The number will definitely be different if the word count is based on meanings of words, as words may develop new meanings simply by semantic changes. Examples of these words are play, train, cast, flat, can, date, book, current, and yard. Resistance can be one of these words. This would be an interesting subject to write about, but it is not the subject of this article. :)

While "resistance" is usually perceived as opposing, confrontational, or undesirable, one may advocate that this word must be perceived as constructive and always stated with positive annotation. Resistance suggests motion, improvement, protection, change, and transformation in the various aspects of life: the physical, thermal, geological, medical, financial, political, biological, social, emotional, organizational, traditional, cultural, theological, and even mental. Resistance is not optional, but necessary.

Resistance is meant to exist and to be used to its fullest. Thus, it has to be wisely managed and may occasionally be reduced but not eliminated; it is not the enemy that must be defeated but a companion needed for success. If resistance is seen this way, some philosophies, strategies, and business will disappear, and there will be a birth of new ones. The only caveat to this concept would exist if we were to live in an absolute vacuum where "resistance to motion" did not exist. This is if an absolute vacuum even exists!

Resistance is one of the essential things in our daily life and presents itself in various forms. If you observe any of the electronic components in your home, office, or vehicle, you would at least spot a resistor. Resistors are the most fundamental and commonly used of all the electronic components and are taken almost for granted. The uses and applications of a resistor within an electrical circuit are vast and varied, with virtually every electronic circuit that was ever designed utilizing one or more types of resistors. They are placed there to "resist"/regulate the flow of current/voltage.

There is a resistance to any moving object around us, a resistance that we call friction. One would wonder what might happen if there were no friction! Once an object is placed in motion, it is easier to keep it in motion; it will always need a resistor to slow it down, turn it, or stop it. Car brakes would be useless with no friction (internal and external); even if a driver jammed on the brakes, a car would never come to a stop. That's dangerous! Without friction, even a simple act such as walking down the road might result in catastrophes. Imagine walking or running on icy or slippery surfaces. Resistance is a necessity for all types of locomotion or movement such as walking, swimming, gliding, galloping, hopping, crawling, and flying. One must; however, acknowledge the value of lubricants to reduce friction in machineries and rotating equipment.

Humans and all other creatures are gifted with immunity or resistance to infection. When a body is invaded by bacteria or viruses, the tissues of the body respond by resisting the poisons of the invader and become immune to them. Bodies with no resistance are eventually dead bodies.

Resistance training such as weightlifting is one of the exercises that provide general health benefits whether it is practiced for training for muscle size or training for strength. The human body is so significant that it adapts to an exercise stimulus after a short period of time (i.e., general adaptation syndrome). One would experience serious gains after training with heavy weights till the body gets ready for new stimulus and "bigger resistance" to breakthrough. Everyone acknowledges this biological mechanism yet struggles to accept a similar concept to other aspects of life associated with other sorts of resistances in life (i.e., resistance to change) that require **MENTAL** resistance training.

Mental resistance training can be practiced in a place that honors a culture of trust, freedom, transparency, fairness, and care. However, it can be very intimidating, uncomfortable, overwhelming, and scary in a place overcome by oppression, domination, captivity, control, and fear. The former place yields to those who freely challenge conventional wisdom and paradigms, those who do not resist change, those who make an impact, while all the latter will yield are puppets, slaves, and clones, and what would be scarier than change for them. They would resist any change.

I have read this profound proverb from an unknown person: "I used to think that bad people did bad things for bad reasons. Now I believe that good people do bad things for seemingly good reasons." Good people possess genuine feelings and desires to keep the whole world a safe world, but they often fail to do enough mental resistance training so they become incapable of analyzing the ever-expanding devastating ideologies, become unprepared to resist them, and unknowingly become assimilated and become part of a world that they despise. What mental resistance training brings includes not only intellect, knowledge, compassion, and understanding, but also freedom, self-respect, confidence, and honor.

Just decide to start mental resistance training, and you need to know that everyone and even the most successful people carry beliefs that are self-limiting. It all boils down to the fear that resides within invisible walls, the walls constructed in our own minds. Sometimes, one has to do what they are most afraid of doing.

Just make sure to resist all of the different information and weigh it using your own mind instead of echoing someone else's mind. You may find out that you are not who you think you are! You may be someone else, and all you need to do to become YOU is resistance.

Challenge Yourself:

- Would you dare to practice mental resistance training by facing different and opposing opinions, beliefs, philosophies, etc.?

Beware: If you are not a voice, you are an echo of those who rule over you, those who you are not allowed to criticize, those who transformed the world into a huge echo-chamber fuelled by fear, prejudice, misunderstanding and intolerance.

Be a Voice, Not an Echo

The words "voice" and "echo" came from Old French *voiz* and from the Greek *echo* respectively for "sound." While voice refers to the sound made by a human, echo refers to a repetition or imitation of sounds. It is amusing to know that the story of Echo is from the Greek mythology. Echo was a nymph who could repeat the last words of others.

The delay in the arrival of any echo is proportional to the distance of the reflecting solid body from the source and the listener. The echo is characterized as a true echo or as reverberation when it is reflected only once, or multiple times respectively. The human ear is capable of detecting and distinguishing between original sounds from echoes, except if the delay of the echo from the original sound is less than 1/10 of a second. This may be OK if voices or echoes are only peaceful sounds.

But the issue becomes critical if these voices or echoes are feelings, opinions, views, plans, dreams, or/and wishes of authors who capitalize on the power of their "voices." Situations, good or bad, may be exaggerated when the role of imitators begins by either producing true echoes or reverberations of the voices of these authors. The voices of authors will always have an impact on their audience, yet this impact varies not because of the contents of the message the voice is carrying, but because of the personalities of listeners.

One may argue that personalities can be described as solid and fluid or may be a mix of the two. "Solids" create great mediums to reflect voices; they are structurally rigid and they have great resistance to change. When a personality becomes "solid," it is expected to have a definite profile with very predictable behavior. Solid personalities may be perceived as slaves of ego, dogma, or a master, or may be seen as consistent and structured behavior.

Fluids' shapes, however, are unpredictable as they take the shape of their finite containers. Human personalities should be fluid in nature (free will suggests so), yet their reactions are unpredictable. Their shapes are hard to determine as their "container" is sized by indeterministic dimensions such as situations, perceptions, experience, feelings, ideologies, etc. An observer may perceive "fluid personalities" as free, flexible, tolerant, and lenient or may be a hypocrite or indecisive.

The greatness of the universe, earth, land, oceans, and mankind comes out of a spectacularly balanced combination of fluids and solids. Where solids resist changes or moves, fluids, in one form or another, make the change. Sailors, just like authors, need fluid (voice - air and water) to sail their boats (message - solid). Galaxies, planets, rockets, planes, trains, cars, etc., need fluids either as a fuel or as a medium to travel through – although some use solid fuels. ;) Any living or moving body needs fluids to function and continue to be alive or moving. Fluids have carried small and gigantic masses. They carry light (!), clouds as well as scents. They carry birds, insects, eggs, and seeds. They carry sand, oceans, and mountains. Not to forget, they could be tornadoes, twisters, and hurricanes. They carry POWER and CHANGE. Solids do not.

No wonder masters of civilizations, ideologies, societies, cultures, organizations, and nations fear what "fluids or voices" may bring. These masters have become or created idols to misguide the masses, use them, exclude their minds, and silence their voices (freeze/solidify their fluids).

Their desire is nothing more than to have a conglomerate of "solid personalities" that possess no voice but an echo, the echo of the voice of a master. Their desire is to keep you "unknown," a mystery to others. People fear the unknown and will end up antagonists living in silos.

Beware: If you are not a voice, you are an echo of those who rule over you, those who you are not allowed to criticize, and those who transformed the world into a huge echo-chamber fuelled by misunderstandings, fear, prejudice, and intolerance.

Ignorance fuelled by Fear = Hate

One's task is not to only voice their minds (if they have one!), but to find all about the silencers to their inner peaceful voice. One would need the courage to conquer the anxiety about voicing their inner voice. In the journey of uncovering these "silencers," beware of those who claim to know The Truth.

The number of people believing in the "untruth" is beyond belief, making the truth relative, circumstantial, and influenced by the perception one has of it: right is wrong, war is peace, losing is winning, an enemy is a friend, wrong is right, and an echo is a voice.

Challenge Yourself:

- Do you know if you are a voice or an echo?
- If a nation/society/individual is controlled, would they be able to objectively analyze situations?
- Can one truly know how much of his/her own voice is voice and not echo?
- Who controls the power to change an individual, a society or a nation?

The quality of life we have today is a result of
the cumulative efforts of people from different times,
different cultures, and different places.

Who Remains!

Out of the billions who have lived, do live, and will live on earth, and out of the seven billion who now live on earth today, who remains? Is it the strongest? Is it the richest? Is it the smartest?

It is only those who left legacies. It is those who are remembered for good things they left behind.

My dear reader, who would you admire and always remember for their great accomplishments? Close your eyes and think about one.

One could admire Einstein for the Theory of Relativity, Newton for his mathematical explanation of light, Edison for electricity application, Avicenna for medicine, and Ibn Al-Haitham for optics, among others. They all saw the fruit of some of their endeavors during their own lives. Today we benefit from their accomplishments and have definitely seen their work in various aspects of our lives. As one observer noted, "They all planted trees for us to harvest."

They all shared similar characteristics. Dedication and the passion to understand and improve the world around them were the motivations for their initiatives.

In some cases, like Einstein's, the physical knowledge gained initially had little application. However, the value of the result was not something tangibly measured, but the satisfaction of a mystery solved, of one more piece of the universe that could be understood.

The scientists who have been contributing to civilization and society resemble only a minute fraction of those who have lived on earth.

One would ask what did those scientists have that you, the respected reader, may or may not have? What you share is potential and what separates us from the greatest minds is how hard we are prepared to work to achieve our dreams.

You may list the qualities or natural characteristics of the achievers and be assured that what you see in them, you can see in yourself when you "operate" at your best. The quality of life that we have today is a result of cumulative efforts of people from different times, different cultures, and different places. You have the potential to contribute to the advancement of civilization and society, and you have the potential to stay as you are. It simply remains for you to make the decision to plant trees for your successors to harvest.

P.S. One may argue that even "extremely bad people" remain. They do remain as a manifestation of evilness and representation of the devil for us to learn from.

Challenge Yourself:

- What is your contribution to humanity?
- Would you be willing to plant trees for others to harvest?

We can only read part of our own life story,
the part that has already been written till this
present moment. We ought to write the rest of our
own story.

Be the Author of Your Own Story

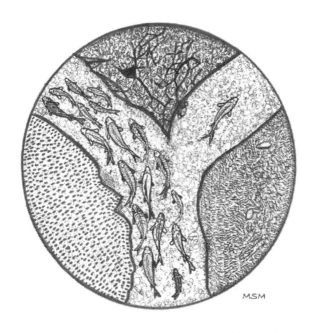

With today's intensely distractive, competitive, challenging, technological, highly informational, and fast-paced environment, it is easy to become so preoccupied with insignificant issues that you lose sight of those things of greater importance. Everyone realizes how critical time is over relationships, growth, efficiency, productivity, compliance, and results. This make "time" is a subject of great interest to discuss and dispute among philosophers, technologists, physicists, psychologists, economists, businessmen, cosmologists, and even religions. Although it may seem very intuitive to some people, it is such a complicated question and an intense mystery to others!!

It looks like there are multiple perspectives of what time is and multiple versions of understandings. These versions are affected by how our senses, cognition, beliefs, and emotions experience the world around us. If this is the case, one would wonder what time is, really. It is something that we deal with every day, and something we all believe we fully understand, yet there is no one simple definition of it. Time is more of a concept than a thing or a substance that you may touch, smell, hear, see, quantify, or even weigh. The word "time" can be used as a noun, an adjective, and a verb and it can represent the past, the present, and the future. It is a multifunctional and very flexible word with various meanings based on its context. All dictionaries relate it to processes, series of events, or periods that are measured in different units (e.g., seconds, minutes, hours, days, weeks, months, etc.).

Philosophers, both ancient and modern, argued over whether time is endless or finite, or real or unreal (e.g., an illusion) respectively. Theologians, on the other hand, believe that the universe must be finite and must have a definite beginning and end. One may ask, what was there before the beginning (i.e., creation)? Was there time then or timelessness? It's a concept that our mind can't comprehend nor be explored by our limited imagination.

Although time is defined by its measurements for physicists, they still consider it as one of the most complicated concepts that had a beginning and hypothetically will end with the universe evolving into empty space. To some, it is fascinating to read about Newtonian time, Relativistic time (Einstein's Theory of Relativity), Time Dilation, Twin Paradox, Arrow of Time, distortion of time, or time travel. **Theoretically** and honoring Einstein's theory, travel through time either forward or backward is possible, just as is the case in travelling between two points in space. However, no one yet has been able to demonstrate or verify it; we only see it in fictional movies, but guess what? There is some theoretical basis to the concept just as is the case in most of fictional old and new movies (e.g., Minority Report, Back to the Future). Whatever the case is, we have been travelling through time and will always move from the past into the future.

Time becomes less definite and the perception of it can significantly be different from one person to another and for the same person during different mental or psychological states. The organs of a human body, for instance, have multiple internal sensors of time (i.e., biological clocks) that keep our organs' function at various paces (heartbeats, eye blinks, etc.).

Our bodies represent a smaller version of a universe, a civilization, a nation, a society, a family, or an organization, and the organs are their entities where everyone has their own rhythm (i.e., clock) that is designed to wonderfully fit the overall magnificent fabric that seamlessly moves towards its destination. Although these clocks can run at different rates or they can halt, the present moment will always be the only moment that is defined as present to all entities.

When travelling, we make sure that we take every important thing we think we'll need for the trip. We regret it if we leave important things behind, don't we? The magnitude of remorse is proportional to the significance of the items left behind. Nations, civilizations, countries, societies, families, organizations, ideologies, technologies, and even individuals travel as bodies (i.e., transform and evolve) through time; they need to ensure that important "organs" are always on board (i.e., similar speeds of motion).

The perception of time is closely connected to motion, all sorts of motions. These motions are made of a string of "present" moments that gets unfolded as time passes. We can only read part of our own life story, the part that has already been written till this present moment. We ought to write the rest of our own story. Otherwise, someone else will not only write it for us but also control our motion, and hopefully, we are not motionless, absent, or travelling "backwards" while everything else moves forwards but us. The greater the difference in the speed of motion is, the greater the gap of progress, growth, or evolution is. Opportunities might not be repeated, and thus you would need to treat every moment as if it were your last.

A quick view through history may clearly demonstrate some real stories about few nations, civilizations, and people. Some have moved forward, while others moved backwards with an ever-increasing gap among them in countless aspects. They all, however, share one common moment: the present. It does not matter who the authors are for these stories; it matters where you want your present to be (i.e., past or future), and if you genuinely want to be the author of the rest of your own story.

Challenge Yourself:

- Imagine a decade passes and your future-self sends your current-self a message! Imagine what that message would be. Would it be a blaming or a thank-you message?

- Were you the author of the last decade of your life or was it someone else?

- You know more details about your life than anybody else. Would you be willing to write it all in a book or would you be selective?

- Can you imagine how your story might be interpreted if it were written in a book?

Bibliography:

Abraham, Ralph and Chris Shaw (1982-1988). Dynamics: the Geometry of Behavior, Parts 1-4, Santa Cruz: Aerial Press.

Abraham, Fred and Combs, Allan (1995). Preface, in Chaos Theory in Psychology, Ed. Abraham and Gilgen, New York: Greenwood.

Bakshi, U. A. and Godse, A. P. (2009).Basic Electronics Engineering. Technical Publications.

Bess F. H., Tharpe A. M., and Gibler A. M. (1986): Case history data on unilaterally impaired children. Ear and hearing.

Bok, Porter, Place & Cronin (2014). Biological Sunscreens Tune Polychromatic Ultraviolet Vision in Mantis Shrimp. Current Biology http://dx.doi.org/10.1016/j.cub.2014.05.071.

Bowmaker J.K. &Dartnall H.J.A. (1980).Visual pigments of rods and cones in a human retina. J. Physiol.

Burnet, C. (1978). The Immune System. San Francisco: FreemanPress.

Cecie Starr (2005). Biology: Concepts and Applications. Thomson Brooks/Cole.

Cladavetscher, A. (1990). Information Integration in the Visual Illusions, in Contributions to Information Integration Theory.Ed. Norman H. Anderson, Hilldale NJ, Erlbaum.

Crick, F. and Mitchison, G. (1986). REM Sleep and Neural Nets, Journal of Mind and Behavior.

CNN.com. "Timeline: A 40-year History of Hacking." Online. (22 Oct.   2003). <http://www.cnn.com/2001/TECH/internet/11/19/hack.history.idg/?related>.

CONOVER, EMILY (July 2016). "Human eye spots single photons". Science News.

Devitt, Michael (June 18, 2001). A Brief History of Computer Hacking, Dynamic Chiropractic, Vol. 19, Issue 13.

Dennett, Daniel (1991). Consciousness Explained, Little, Brown and Co., Boston.

Edson Gary (2009). Masks and Masking: Faces of Tradition and Belief Worldwide. McFarland

Fel, Jade (March 13, 2017).Cybercrime is often thought of as a type of modern warfare, but hacking practices have been around longer than you might expect.Publishedhttps://eandt.theiet.org/content/articles/2017/03/hacking-through-the-years-a-brief-history-of-cyber-crime/.

Freeman, Walter (1993). Societies of Bruins. Hilldale N J: Erlbaum.

Genova, Cathleen (December 13, 2007). Blind humans lacking rods and cones retain normal responses to non-visual effects of light. Cell Press.

Goertzel, B. (1991). "Quantum Theory and Consciousness," Journal of Mind and Behavior.

Hancock, Claire (2012). The Titanic Notebook: The Story of the World's Most Famous Ship. Insight Editions.

Hartmann, E. (1991). Boundaries in the Mind. New York: Basic.

Hebb, Donald (1948). The Organization of Behavior. New York: Wiley.

How Do You Know If an Animal Can See Color?,https://askabiologist.asu.edu/colors-animals-see

Jameson, K. A.; Highnote, S. M. & Wasserman, L. M. (2001)."Richer color experience in observers with multiple photo-pigment opsin genes". Psychonomic Bulletin and Review.

J. Alan Hobson, Edward F. Pace-Scott, & Robert Stickgold (2000), "Dreaming and the brain: Toward a cognitive neuroscience of conscious states", Behavioral and Brain Sciences 23.

Kaga, K. and Asato, H. (2013). Microtia and Atresia: Combined Approach by Plastic and Otologic Surgery, Karger Medical and Scientific Publishers.

Kapleau, Philip (1980). The Three Pillars of Zen. New York: Doubleday.

Kaiser, Ward (2013).How Maps Change Things, Wood Lake Publications.

Keesing Richard. A Brief History of Isaac Newton's Apple Tree, https://www.york.ac.uk/physics/about/newtonsappletree/.

Levy, Steven (1984).Hacking Heroes of the Computer Revolution. Garden City, N.Y. Anchor/Doubleday.

Mersey, Lord (1999). The Loss of the Titanic, 1912.The Stationery Office.

Minahan, James (2000). One Europe, many nations: a historical dictionary of European national groups. Greenwood Publishing Group.

Monmonier, Mark (2004).Rhumb Lines and Map Wars: A Social History of the Mercator Projection, University of Chicago Press.

Nosowitz, Dan(June 01, 2015). Why Thousands of New Animal Species Are Still Discovered Each Year https://www.atlasobscura.com/articles/new-animal-species.

Redd, Nola Taylor.Einstein's Theory of General Relativity.https://www.space.com/17661-theory-general-relativity.html

Rods and Cones of the Human Eye, https://askabiologist.asu.edu/rods-and-cones

Seife, Charles (2000). Zero: The Biography of a Dangerous Idea, Penguin Group, NY, USA.

Silber MH, Ancoli-Israel S, Bonnet MH, Chokroverty S, Grigg-Damberger MM, Hirshkowitz M, Kapen S, Keenan SA, Kryger MH, Penzel T, Pressman MR, Iber C (March 2007). "The visual scoring of sleep in adults" .Journal of Clinical Sleep Medicine. 3 (2): 121–131.

Slatalla, Michelle (28 Oct. 2003). A Brief History of Hacking. Online. Discovery Communications.http://tlc.discovery.com/convergence/hackers/articles/history.html.

"Sleep-Wake Cycle: Its Physiology and Impact on Health" (2006). National Sleep Foundation.

Snyder J.P. Cartography in the Renaissance in The History of Cartography, Volume 3, part I, p365.

Suplee, Curt (January12, 2000), The History of Zero. https://www.washingtonpost.com/archive/2000/01/12/the-history-of-zero/36a6a2fd-9e18-484d-ae6f-450af0340830/?noredirect=on&utm_term=.d0f408f69dca.

The incredible – and bizarre – spectrum of animal colour vision (11 March 2016), COSMOS, The Science of Everything, https://cosmosmagazine.com/biology/incredible-bizarre-spectrum-animal-colour-vision.

Tymieniecka, A-T. (2003): Does the World exist? Plurisignificant Ciphering of Reality. Kluwer Academy Publications.

University of Cambridge (February 12, 2014). Surgical implants: Implant stiffness is a major cause of foreign body reaction. Science Daily.

https://www.sciencedaily.com/releases/2014/02/140212132805.htm

Whorf, Benjamin Lee (1949). Language, Thought and Reality. Cambridge: MIT Press

Williams, Zev (Sep 20, 2012). "Inducing Tolerance to Pregnancy".
New England Journal of Medicine. 367: 1159–1161

Wölfel, Matthias; McDonough, John (2009).Distant Speech
Recognition. Chichester: John Wiley & Sons. p. 48.

Woodward, D. and Harley J.B. (1987), The History of
Cartography, Volume 3, Cartography in the European
Renaissance, University of Chicago.

Acknowledgements

Turning an idea into a book is not as easy as it may sound and as much pride a publication of a book brings as much responsibilities come with it.

I just want to say to my respected readers that this book was not only a result of my own thoughts and work but there were many invisible human-angels who helped me in various stages. For those who have supported me in any way since I started in this journey, you all know who you are, I am truly grateful for support, guidance and criticism.

First and foremost, I would like to thank God almighty for giving me what it takes to write this book. I would like also to thank the individuals that helped make it happen.

I am deeply indebted to Abdul-Jaleel Khalifah for his thorough review of the book, suggestions and criticism.

I owe an enormous debt of gratitude to those who read the book and gave me very generous reviews, insightful guidance and reflections. They are Dr. Marshall Goldsmith, Dr. Heather Younger and Bruce Kasanoff.

I very much appreciate the efforts of Mohammed Al-Dawood, Susan Rooks and John Keszler to edit the contents of book.

I am also immensely grateful to the four artists who contributed to the success of the completion of the artwork in the book namely, Furqan Ahmed Qidwai for the development of the book cover; and the greatest young artists, my kids, Mahmoud, Zainab and Sharaf for creating very remarkable and thought provoking artwork. I am really impressed by every single piece of their arts.

During the journey of writing this book, I was very lucky to have a great support, guidance and encouragement from two of my dear friends, Nabeel Al Habib and Bob Sullivan.

My acknowledgement is not complete without thanking the biggest source of my aspiration and strength, my loving wife, May, my mirror, critic, and my very best companion.

The only ones that I could not thank them personally, are those great artists who developed or possess the copy rights of 1 illustration that I used in one article: Blinking Minds. This illustration is available in numerous sites, yet I did make all the efforts to seek their permissions but could not.

The last appreciation message is given to you, the reader of this book. I hope you have enjoyed reading the book and have found some gems to treasure.

I must conclude by affirming that that this book and its contents strictly reflect my own ideas and perceptions that I wanted to write about and share with others.

About the Author

Saeed Mubarak Saeed is a thought provoking author who has published tens of articles to promote innovation and challenge conventional wisdom. His contribution is a blend of many volunteer activities that cover a wide spectrum of social, cultural, educational and technical to complement conventional school, social and cultural approaches to add greater value and better quality to individuals, communities and corporations. His motto is "Challenge Paradigm – Make Impact" which has been cultivated in many initiatives and programs he leads. Among these programs are: "Let's Learn", "Dream- Believe-Achieve", "What's my Dream", "who Remains?" and "Blood Donation".

Saeed is a recognized technical and inspirational author and speaker demonstrating the significance of digital energy. He has been among the society of petroleum engineers' international distinguished lecturer, a panelist, keynote, invited speaker and discussion leader of in numerous events in 20 counties including technical conferences, workshops, forums and symposia.

Saeed has twenty-seven years of Petroleum Industry and has served the industry in various capacities that span across local and international levels, technical and administrative, simple to leadership roles.

His contributions to the area of Intelligent Energy and innovation were recognized by renowned technical, governmental and social authorities. He is recipient of several national, regional and international awards related to his innovative contribution to the area of intelligent fields including the 2009 SPE Regional Management and Information award, 2012 World Oil Innovative Thinker award, 2013 King's award for innovation, the 2014 SPE international award for management and information, the international 2019 SPE Distinguished Service Award, and the 2019 SPE Distinguished member award. He also earned the 2011/2012 SPE Saudi Section "Community Service Award" for his contribution to Social programs. He was a finalist in 2016 WorldOil Lifetime Achievement award.

Saeed is currently the company Intelligent Fields focus area champion at Saudi Aramco, based in Dhahran, Saudi Arabia. He serves as the Chairman of Digital Energy Technical Section (DETS), a member in the SPE International M&I (Management and Information) awards advisory committee, a member in the SPE DSEA advisory Committee.

Saeed holds a bachelor degree in Chemical engineering and a master degree in petroleum engineering.

Made in the USA
Monee, IL
26 February 2020